BASKETBALL'S PRO-SET PLAYBOOK:

The Complete Offensive Arsenal

Previous Books by the Author:

Complete Book of Zone Game Basketball
Coach's Guide to Basketball's 1-4 Offense
Pressure Game Basketball
Seven Championship-Tested Basketball Offenses
Tempo-Control Basketball
Successful Team Techniques in Basketball

BASKETBALL'S PRO-SET PLAYBOOK:

The Complete Offensive Arsenal

Harry L. "Mike" Harkins

Parker Publishing Company, Inc. West Nyack, New York

Library of Congress Cataloging in Publication Data

Harkins, Harry L.
  Basketball's pro-set playbook.

  Includes index.
  1. Basketball—Offense. 2. Basketball coaching.
I. Title
GV889.H33   796.32'32   82-3487
ISBN 0-13-056366-8   AACR2

Printed in the United States of America

Dedication

To the future of the Harkins family:

Michael Vincent Harkins, and his wife Diane
Patrice Harkins
James Fenton Harkins
Shellee Ann Harkins
Jamee Cameron Harkins

What Basketball's Pro-Set Playbook Offers

This book provides you with an in-depth, detailed account of basketball's most successful offense. It has been the offense of championship teams at all levels. The great UCLA teams of John Wooden used this set almost exclusively and popularized it nationwide. Since that time, it has been adopted by numerous high school and college teams. However, I choose to call this book, *Basketball's Pro-Set Playbook: The Complete Offensive Arsenal* because I feel the professional teams have, through necessity, developed it to the fullest. It is the offensive set of the majority of the NBA teams.

There are two primary reasons for this: First, since professional teams play so many games, they are forced to find a set that allows for a great deal of adaptation and change. Putting the post man at the free throw line opens up the ballside lay-up area and facilitates a wide variety of play situations. Second, the offense is adaptable to a vast range of personnel alignments. It is not as necessary to have the dominant post man. Since most professional teams have great players at guard and forward but dominant post men are at a premium, the use of this offense by professional teams is almost universal.

These same offensive problems of finding functional play situations that best utilize the abilities of our players plague all of us who coach basketball. The pro-set basketball playbook will provide some ideas that will ease this problem for you.

This is an offensive playbook composed of plays run from the pro-set. The number of plays included in this book is far too great to use in one season and probably in a coaching career. The intent is to provide a wide variety of choices from which to design your offense. The broad scope of material offers an opportunity to find specific plays that fit a given coaching situation; plays that may allow you to take advantage of the talents of your personnel and either hide or compensate for their weaknesses.

The plays that compose the offense are found in the first seven chapters. They are organized by their play keys in the following order.

Chapter 1: "Inside Cut Plays"

An "Inside Cut" occurs when a guard passes to the forward on his side of the court and cuts inside him. The fundamental feature of the two-guard, high-post offense is the inside cut play. The guard, passing to his forward and slashing off the high-post man, is the basic move of this play because of the uncomplicated scoring potential it affords. From the forward position, the ball can be moved with one short, safe pass to the corner, high post, low post, or to the point. The availability of these passing outlets opens up the potential for a myriad of scoring options. This chapter presents a great number of inside cut plays.

Chapter 2: "Outside Cut Plays"

An "Outside Cut" ensues when a guard passes to the forward on his side of the court and cuts outside of him. The outside cut play is a very functional move because it engages the primary defensive pressure player (onside forward) and the primary defensive help player (offside forward) of the interior of the defense. Since the defensive post man is forced to play high to cover the offensive high-post man, much lay-up potential is created. This movement especially facilitates plays that include crosscourt lob passes and opportunities for the offside forward to come across the lane and post up.

Chapter 3: "Dribble Entry Plays"

When a guard dribbles at a forward to clear him away and assume his position, the "Dribble Entry" is initiated. The dribble entry play is very valuable to a team that must face strong defensive pressure. It allows the ball to be moved to the very strategic forward position without the necessity of a pass.

Chapter 4: "Plays Keyed by a Guard-to-Guard Pass"

Guard-to-guard passes are becoming more important because the pressure-and-help man-to-man defense makes penetration passes (guard-to-forward or guard-to-post man) very difficult. This chapter contains plays that are keyed by a guard-to-guard pass.

Chapter 5: "Plays Keyed by a Pass to the Post"

The "Pass-to-the-Post" play has many functions. It may be used to take the defensive pressure off the onside forward, feed the low-post positions, engage the defensive post man, or create a lot of movement by splitting the post. The plays in this chapter include maneuvers that will allow you to choose the ones that best fit your personnel.

Chapter 6: "Plays Keyed by a Diagonal Cut"

A "Diagonal Cut" results when a guard passes to the forward on his side and cuts diagonally down the free throw lane. It is very functional for teams with a strong post man because the direction of the cut temporarily hinders the offside help and provides a time to work post-oriented plays.

Chapter 7: "Double-Cut Plays"

The "Double Cut" is effected when the offensive guard passes to his forward, and both offensive guards cut through.

The idea of sending both guards through simultaneously has much merit. Among its attributes are: (1) it removes the saggers and helpers from the front of the defense; (2) it makes it difficult for the opponents to fast break because their potential outlet men are in adverse introductory positions, and (3) it doubles the number of initial cutters who must be covered. However, since one guard is usually the primary player responsible for defensive balance, much time must be spent defining this duty.

Chapter 8: "Man-to-Man Pressure Relievers"

"Pressure Relievers" are individual and team maneuvers designed to counter defensive pressure. This chapter provides plays, options, and maneuvers that take advantage of defensive pressure.

Chapter 9: "Versus Zone Defenses"

Some of the plays in the first seven chapters are functional against zone defenses. Chapter Nine details the adaptations that make them work.

Chapter 10: "Evaluating the Pro-Set Offense"

The strengths and weaknesses of the offense are analyzed in terms of the fundamentals of man-to-man offense.

The Pro-Set Offense is one of the great basketball offenses. The materials in this book can be used by coaches at all levels to help them design a successful offensive plan.

Harry L. "Mike" Harkins

Acknowledgments

Special tribute goes to my wife, Grace, for the hours of typing (and her ability to decipher my handwritten manuscript) and for her meticulous efforts on the diagrams.

Grateful appreciation is also expressed to the sources of my basketball knowledge, including:

Russ Estey and Mike Krino, my high school coaches;
Russ Beichly and Red Cochrane, my college coaches;
The players who have played on my teams;
And the publishers of *The Coaching Clinic, Scholastic Coach, Coach and Athlete,* and *Athletic Journal.*

A final note of thanks goes to my number one fans (and granddaughters), Shellee Ann and Jamee Cameron Harkins.

H. L. H.

Contents

Contents

BASKETBALL'S PRO-SET PLAYBOOK:

The Complete Offensive Arsenal

1

INSIDE CUT PLAYS

The fundamental play of the two-guard high-post offense is the inside cut play. The guard passing to his forward and slashing off the high-post man is very basic because of its uncomplicated scoring potential. From the forward position the ball can be moved with one short, safe pass to the corner, high post, low post, or to the point. The availability of these passing outlets opens up the potential for a myriad of scoring options. Following is a wide variety of inside cut plays.

THE BASIC UCLA PLAY

The most often-used play from this formation is the one made famous by UCLA. This play begins as (1) passes to (3) and slashes off (5) to the ballside lay-up area. If the guard is a strong player with his back to the basket, he may post up at this point and (3) will attempt to get him the ball for a one-on-one play. This is illustrated in Diagram 1-1.

If (2)'s defensive man jams the high post area, he must clear him by moving as shown in Diagram 1-2.

(3) then passes to (5) and down screens for (1), who

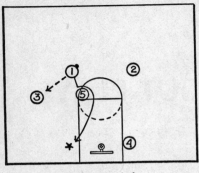

Diagram 1-1

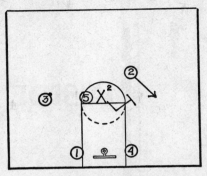

Diagram 1-2

brushes by the screen and moves out for a possible jump shot. See Diagram 1-3.

Upon receiving the ball, (5) pivots toward the basket, looks first for (1) moving out and then inside for forwards (3) and (4). Many teams try hard to get the ball to (1) coming out, but the percentage play is to get the ball inside to one of the forwards. (3) must screen and then roll inside and (4) must keep his eye on (5) and move in the lane as soon as (5) looks at him. Both (3) and (4) must establish an angle on their opponent and give (5) a target away from the defender. See Diagram 1-4.

If nothing develops, (1) and (2) move out front, the ball is given to one of them, and a new play is keyed.

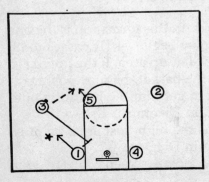

Diagram 1-3

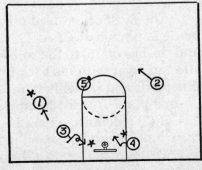

Diagram 1-4

SPECIAL OPTIONS

Following are some options that may be added to the basic UCLA play to give it depth or to handle special situations.

The Swing-It Option

In this option, (1) again cuts through after passing to (3); (3) again passes to (5) and down screens for (1); (3) and (4) then post up as (1) moves out for the possible jump shot. See Diagrams 1-5 and 1-6.

Particularly notice in Diagram 1-6 that this time, (5) stepped out more toward the head of the key to receive the ball from (3). He again looked for (1) moving out, (3) rolling to post up, and (4) moving in the lane.

When using the swing-it option, the idea is to take advantage of (4)'s defender. In most cases, this defender would be playing ballside and either three-quarters or fronting. To capitalize on X4's defensive position, (5) fakes to (4) to pull X4 up, and then passes to (2). (2) now has a passing angle that allows (4) to catch the ball inside of X4 for a power lay-up. See Diagrams 1-7 and 1-8 for this maneuver.

If (2) cannot get the ball in to (4), the post man (5) screens down for the offside forward [(3) in Diagram 1-9] who breaks to the free throw line.

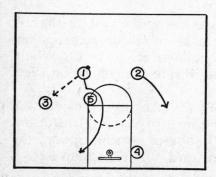

Diagram 1-5

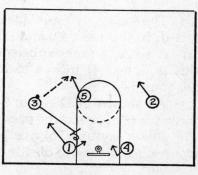

Diagram 1-6

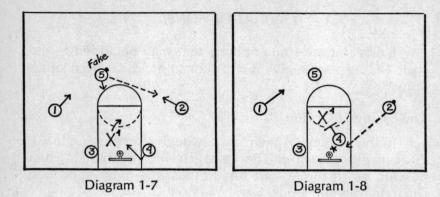

Diagram 1-7   Diagram 1-8

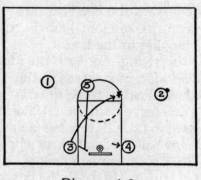

Diagram 1-9

The same "swing-it" idea can be used to post (2), the tall guard. In this case, (2) and (4) make an offside exchange on (1)'s slash cut and the subsequent down screen by (3). When this is done, (4) moves to the offside wing position. See Diagram 1-10.

As shown in Diagram 1-11, (5) fakes to (2) inside and passes to (4) who has the passing angle to pass to (2) inside for the power lay-up. To give (4) another passing option, (5) again screens for the offside forward, (3) in Diagram 1-12.

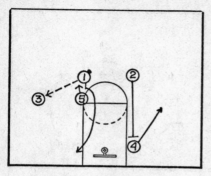

Diagram 1-10

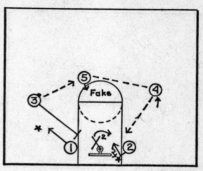

Diagram 1-11

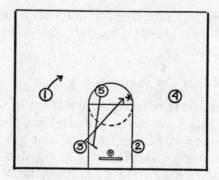

Diagram 1-12

Inside Cut Backdoor Option

An option that works very well when used in conjunction with the "swing-it" idea is the inside cut backdoor play.

(1) passes to (3) and makes his inside cut. At the same time, (2) drifts to the offside wing area. See Diagram 1-13.

(3) passes to (5) as he steps out to the top of the circle. (5) fakes a pass to (2) which causes (2)'s defender to overplay him. This fake also tells (4) to break toward the ball. (5) passes to (4) who looks for (2) backdooring his man. (3) screens down

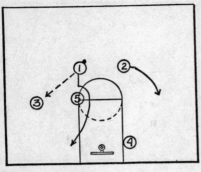

Diagram 1-13

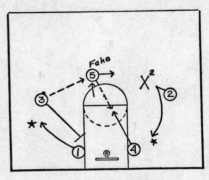

Diagram 1-14

for (1) and (1) breaks to the free throw line extended. This gives (5) another option and keeps the defenders on that side busy. See Diagram 1-14.

The Post Backdoor Option

An option that may be run when (3) cannot get the ball to (5) is the post backdoor move. After (1) has passed to (3) and made his slashing cut off (5), (3) cannot get the ball to (5) because (5) is being overplayed. Seeing this, (1) clears the ballside low-post area and loops around the offside forward, (4), as Diagram 1-15 shows. (5) then backdoors X5 and cuts to the basket. See Diagram 1-16.

If (5) is not open, (2), who had drifted away from the play, cuts back to the head of the key, takes a pass from (3), and passes it quickly to (1) coming around (4). See Diagram 1-17.

THE POST EXCHANGE PLAY

The post exchange play occurs when (5) waits for (1)'s cut through [after (1)'s pass to (3)] and then exchanges with the offside forward. See Diagrams 1-18 and 1-19.

(3) then passes to (4) and the same options prevail as with the UCLA play. See Diagram 1-20.

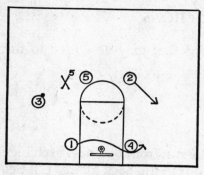

Diagram 1-15

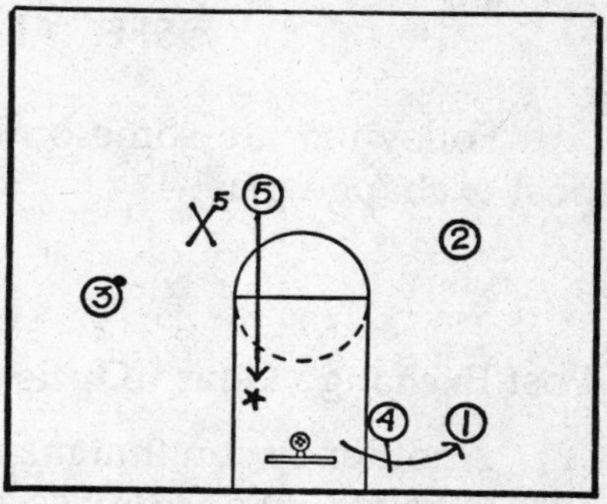

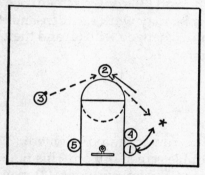

Diagram 1-16

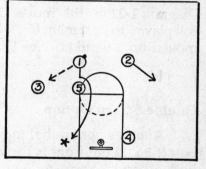

Diagram 1-17

Diagram 1-18

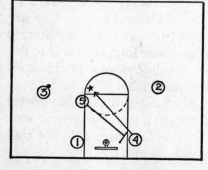

Diagram 1-19

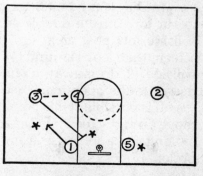

Diagram 1-20

SPECIAL OPTIONS

Following are some options that may be added to the post exchange play.

Post Exchange Guard Option

Another option that may be run from this post exchange idea is keyed when (3) passes out to the back guard, (2). See Diagram 1-21.

When this option is run, (2) may do one of two things. He may pass to (1) coming toward him off (3)'s down screen. See Diagram 1-22 for this move. Or, he may work a screen-and-roll play with post man, (5), who exchanged with (4) and then moved up toward (2). See Diagram 1-23.

Double Screen Option

Another option that may be run at the point where (3) passes to (2) out front is the double screen option. This time both (3) and (4) screen down for (1), who pops out. (2) may pass to (1) coming out, or reverse it to (5), who moved out expecting the pass. See Diagram 1-24.

In Diagram 1-24, (2) reversed the ball to (5). This tells (1) to cut low off the double screen of (3) and (4), and to the ballside low-post area. (3), the bottom man of the double screen, then loops around (4), free throw line-high and to the ballside. (2) drifts away to remove the defensive sagger and (5) passes to the open man. See Diagram 1-25.

It is possible at this point to add a lob option by having (4) move up and screen for (2), who cuts to the offside lay-up area looking for a lob pass from (5). See Diagram 1-26 for this option.

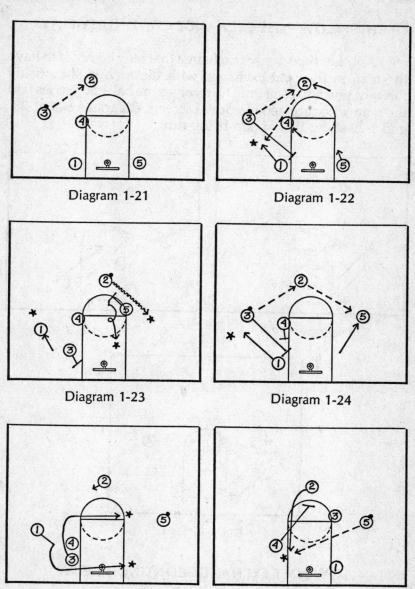

Diagram 1-21

Diagram 1-22

Diagram 1-23

Diagram 1-24

Diagram 1-25

Diagram 1-26

HIGH-LOW POST EXCHANGE CONTINUITY PLAY

Another type of post exchange that may be run is to have the man in the post exchange with the man in the offside forward position each time he receives the ball and passes it to the man who received the down screen. Diagrams 1-27, 1-28, and 1-29 show this option being run.

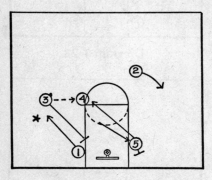

Diagram 1-27

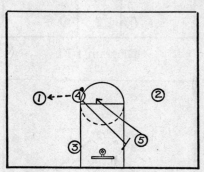

Diagram 1-28

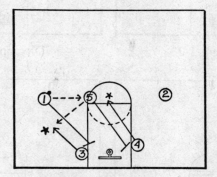

Diagram 1-29

LOW-POST EXCHANGE CONTINUITY PLAY

(1) has slashed through and (3) passes to (5) and down screens for (1). (5) steps out to receive the ball. See Diagram 1-30.

When (5) passes to (1), coming out for the possible jump shot, (3), instead of posting up, continues across the lane and screens for (4) who comes to the ballside. See Diagram 1-31.

If (4) is not open, (5) again steps out and receives the ball from (1), who down screens for (4). See Diagram 1-32.

(5) then passes to (4) and (1) screens away for (3), who comes to the ball. See Diagram 1-33.

It is important for (2) to clear away when (5) receives the ball. If he does not, his defender can often blindside (5) and steal the ball. To keep X2 honest, a backdoor play may be added. Using the starting position shown in Diagram 1-33, (5) keys the backdoor by faking to (2). This tells (3) to come to the

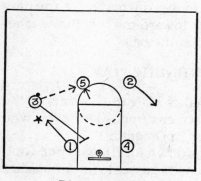

Diagram 1-30

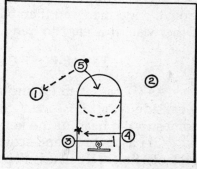

Diagram 1-31

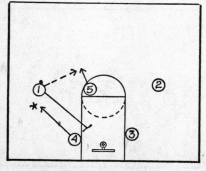

Diagram 1-32

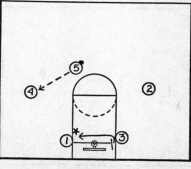

Diagram 1-33

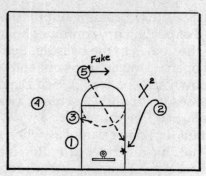

Diagram 1-34

ballside, (1) not to screen opposite, and also tells (2) to back-door X2. See Diagram 1-34.

It is also important that (5) moves out to receive any pass from a wing man and then back toward the free throw lane. Otherwise, it is easy to deny him the ball.

TRIPLE-POST CONTINUITY PLAY

As (1) passes to (3) and makes his cut, (2) clears to the weakside wing. Post man (5) screens opposite for (4), who comes to the head of the key as in Diagram 1-35.

(3) passes to (4) and screens down for (1), who pops out. (4) looks first at (1); if he isn't open, he passes to (2) and slashes off (5), who has moved back up to the high post. See Diagram 1-36.

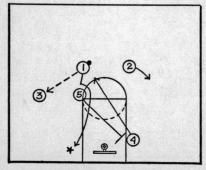

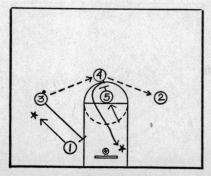

Diagram 1-35   Diagram 1-36

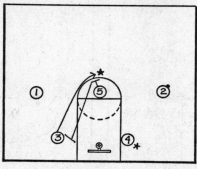

Diagram 1-37

After (4) slashes by, (5) screens opposite for (3), who comes to the head of the key. See Diagram 1-37. The play is then repeated.

THE MULTI-OPTION POST EXCHANGE PLAY

This play starts with (1) making his inside cut and (5) screening for (4), the offside forward. See Diagram 1-38 for illustration of this play.

This time, however, (1) clears to the ballside corner and (4) swings to the ballside low-post area as shown in Diagram 1-39.

If nothing has developed, (3) passes to (5), who has moved back to the top of the key. (5) looks first for (2) on a

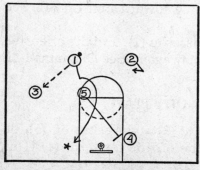

Diagram 1-38

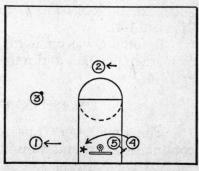

Diagram 1-39

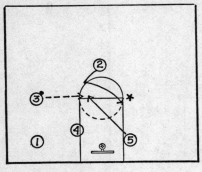

Diagram 1-40

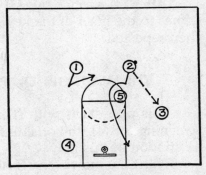

Diagram 1-41

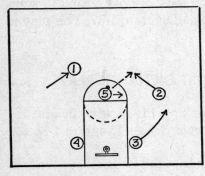

Diagram 1-42

Diagram 1-43

backdoor-type move. (2) sets this up by moving toward the ball. See Diagram 1-40.

If (2) isn't open, (5) looks for (3) cutting off a screen set by (4). Next, he looks for (1) cutting toward him off (4). See Diagram 1-41.

If nothing was open, (5) passes to (2), and the offensive men are in position to run the play again. See Diagrams 1-42 and 1-43.

SLASH CONTINUITY PLAY

This time, after (1) passes to (3) and slashes off (5), he continues down and around the offside forward, (4). This leaves room in the ballside low-post area for (5) to swing down and post low. See Diagram 1-44.

As soon as it is apparent (5) cannot receive the ball in the low-post area, (4) cuts to the ballside high-post area. If he receives the ball, he may shoot or look for (5) inside. (5) is open quite often in this situation because his man is usually over-playing him and often fronts him. See Diagram 1-45.

If (3) cannot get the ball to (4), he passes to (2), who reverses the ball to (1). (2) then slash-cuts off (4) to the ballside post area and the play is repeated. See Diagram 1-46 and note that (3) moved out front after (2) cut through.

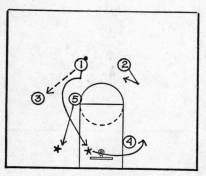

Diagram 1-44

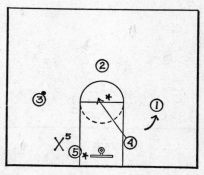

Diagram 1-45

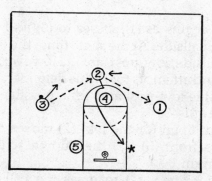

Diagram 1-46

REVERSE OR SPLIT PLAY

A very similar play may be run that eliminates the inside pivot man rotation and adds a split option. After (1) has passed to (3), slashed through and then cleared, (5) swings low and two options are available: (3) may again pass to (2), who reverses the ball to (1) (as in Diagram 1-47); or (3) may pass to (5) inside and split the post with (2) (as in Diagram 1-48).

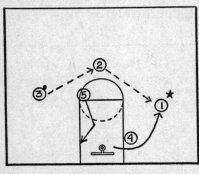

Diagram 1-47

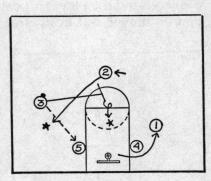

Diagram 1-48

GUARD LOB PLAY

This play begins as (1) passes to (3) and starts to slash through on the ballside. At the same time, the offside forward cuts to the ballside low-post area. However, (1) fakes the ballside slash and attempts to rub his defender off on (5), as he cuts to the offside low-post area for a possible lob pass from (3). See Diagram 1-49.

If (1) is not open for the lob, (2) moves to the ball and receives a pass from (3). (3) then down screens for (4) as shown in Diagram 1-50.

If (4) is not open, (2) reverses the ball to (1), who is moving out to the wing area. (4) then cuts off (3) to the ballside

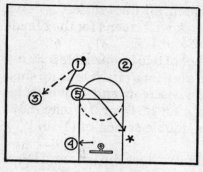

Diagram 1-49

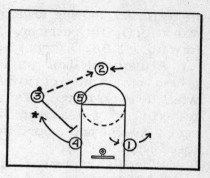

Diagram 1-50

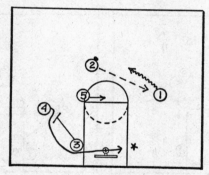

Diagram 1-51

low-post area, and (1) attempts to pass to him. If nothing develops, (1) dribbles out front and another play is run. See Diagram 1-51.

WEAKSIDE, POST-DOWN PLAY

At times, plays are run on the side opposite the post man. These are called weakside plays.

This play begins when (1), the guard away from the post man, passes to his forward, (3), and cuts through to the low-post area. (3) looks first to (1), posting inside, then passes to guard, (2), moving toward him. (3) then makes a down screen for (1). The post man, (5), down screens for the offside forward, (4). See Diagrams 1-52 and 1-53.

At this point (1) can run either of two options: He may use (3)'s screen and move out to the wing for a possible jump shot, which tells (4) to use (5)'s down screen and move to his respective wing area (as in Diagram 1-54); or, (1) may move across the lane and around the double screen of (4) and (5). (See Diagram 1-55.)

When this happens, (4) moves across the lane and loops around (3) for a possible jump shot in Diagram 1-56.

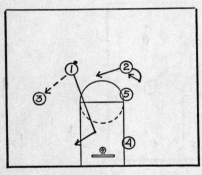

Diagram 1-52

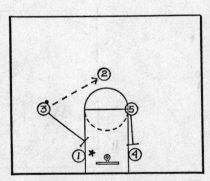

Diagram 1-53

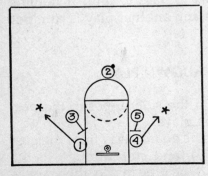

Diagram 1-54

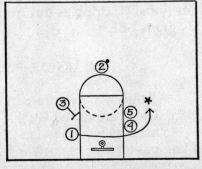

Diagram 1-55

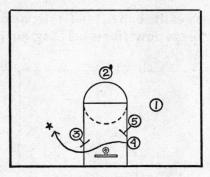

Diagram 1-56

If either (1) or (4) receive the ball, they may shoot or look for the man posting on their side.

SPECIAL OPTION

The Quick Option

An option off this play is to have (3), upon receiving the ball from (1), pass it quickly to (2). (1) then makes his cut to the ballside post and waits as (4) steps out of his down screen from (5). See Diagram 1-57.

If (2) cannot get the ball to (4), (1) then cuts across the lane and under (5). This tells (4) to cut over (5) and look for a pass from (2). See Diagram 1-58.

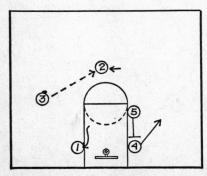

Diagram 1-57

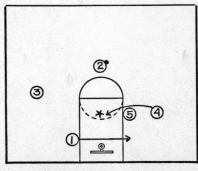

Diagram 1-58

If (2) cannot get the ball to (4), (1) steps out of (5)'s down screen and (3) screens down for (4) as Diagram 1-59 illustrates.

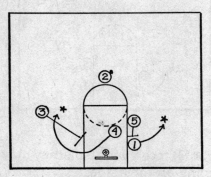

Diagram 1-59

2 ‖ OUTSIDE CUT PLAYS

The outside cut play is a very functional move because it engages the primary defensive pressure player (onside forward) and the primary defensive help player (offside forward) in the defensive interior. Since the defensive post is forced to play high to cover the offensive high post, much lay-up potential is created. The outside cut especially facilitates plays that include crosscourt lob passes and opportunities for the offside forward to come across the lane and "post up."

FORWARD LOB PLAY

Probably the most often-used outside cut play works as follows. Guard (1) passes to his forward, (3), and makes an outside cut. The offside forward, (4), moves to the ballside low-post area for a possible one-on-one play. See Diagram 2-1.

(3) then returns the ball to (1) and cuts over the blind screen set by post man, (5), for a possible lob pass. See Diagram 2-2.

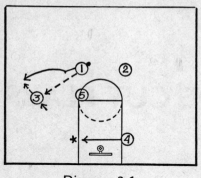

Diagram 2-1

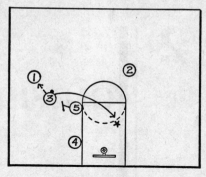

Diagram 2-2

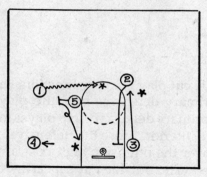

Diagram 2-3

If (3) or (4) are not open, (4) clears to the corner and (1) works a screen-and-roll play with (5) as shown in Diagram 2-3.

At the same time (2) screens for (3) and (3) moves out front. This keeps the offside defense busy.

Post-Down Option

A slight variation that may be run off the basic play occurs at the point when (3) hands the ball back to (1). This tells the high post, (5), to move to the ballside low post and the offside forward, (4), to break to the ballside high post. See Diagram 2-4.

From there, the options are the same, even though the positions of the players are changed. See Diagram 2-5 and Diagram 2-6.

This variation helps prevent the offense from being too easy to diagnose.

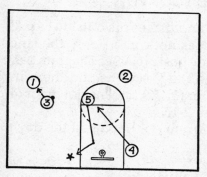

Diagram 2-4

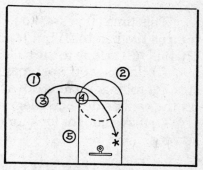

Diagram 2-5

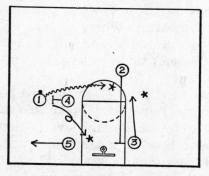

Diagram 2-6

FORWARD ACROSS PLAY

This time, after (1) has made his outside cut and received a return pass from (3), (3) cuts down and across the lane to form a natural screen for (4). (4) uses the screen and cuts to the ballside post area. See Diagram 2-7.

If (4) is not open, (1) dribbles off (5). This clears (4) to the corner and tells (2) to screen down for (3). (1) may shoot or hit the open man, as in Diagram 2-8.

THE FORWARD LOOP PLAY

This time (1) passes to (3) and makes his outside cut. (3) returns the ball to (1) but (4) does not come across the lane. This tells (3) to loop to the ballside post area. See Diagram 2-9.

(1) dribbles off post man, (5). (5) screens and then, instead of rolling, screens down for (3). (2) screens down for (4) on the weak side. See Diagram 2-10.

(1) may shoot or look for (3) and (4) coming off the down screens.

LOW-POST ISOLATION PLAY

This play begins when guard, (1), passes to forward, (3), and makes an outside cut. (3) returns the ball to (1) and cuts over the high-post man, (5). The offside forward, (4), swings to the ballside low-post area where his man will front him or at least play him very strong to one side. See Diagram 2-11.

Note that (2) clears to the other side to take his defender out of the play.

(1) then fakes a pass to (4) in the low post to force the overplay. This time, however, (3) fakes his cut to the basket and comes back to the head of the key. (1) then passes to (3). (3) is usually open because his defender was very aware of the possible lob pass. See Diagram 2-12.

(4) pins his defender by backing into him and receives a pass from (3) for a power lay-up. See Diagram 2-13.

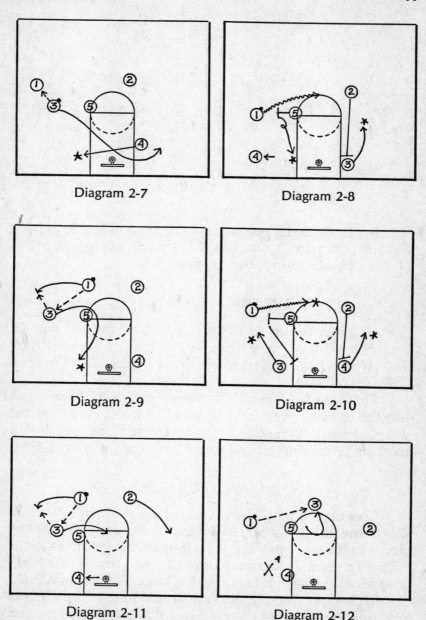

Diagram 2-7

Diagram 2-8

Diagram 2-9

Diagram 2-10

Diagram 2-11

Diagram 2-12

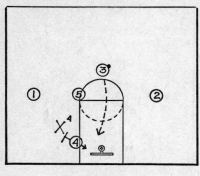

Diagram 2-13

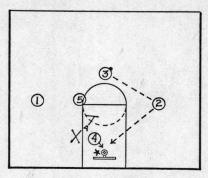

Diagram 2-14

If (4)'s defender gets around the pin and is able to front him, (3) passes to (2), who then has the angle to get the ball to (4) for a power lay-up. See Diagram 2-14.

THE DOUBLE LOB PLAY

(1) again passes to (3) and makes an outside cut. (3) returns the ball to (1) and cuts over the double screen set by (5) and (4) who have moved across the lane, shown in Diagram 2-15.

This time, however, (2) moves toward (1) and receives an outside handoff from him. (1) hands off and cuts over the double screen. (2) may lob pass to (1) (see Diagram 2-16), or look for (3) coming around (5) and (4) (see Diagram 2-17).

DELAYED LOB PLAY

This time, after (3) hands off to (1), he cuts in a direction that forms a natural screen for high-post man, (5), sliding down to the low-post. If (5) is not open, he continues to the ballside corner. At the same time, (3) loops back to the high-post area and (4) moves across the lane. See Diagram 2-18.

(1) hands off to (2), moving toward him, and then goes over the double screen formed by (3) and (4). See Diagram 2-19.

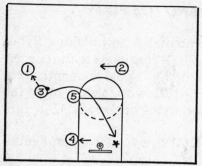

Diagram 2-15

Diagram 2-16

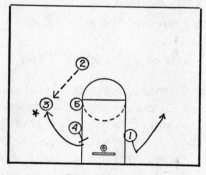

Diagram 2-17

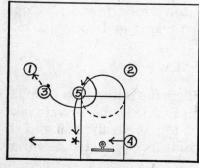

Diagram 2-18

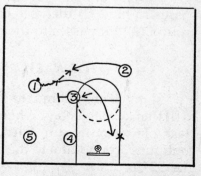

Diagram 2-19

FORWARD FAKE AND LOB PLAY

This time, (1) passes to (3) and makes his outside cut, but (3) fakes to him and keeps the ball. (1) continues to the corner. At the same time, (4) moved to the high-post area and along with (5) formed a double screen for (2), who faked a cut to the ball and went over the screen and to the basket. See Diagram 2-20.

If the lob is not made to (2), (4) steps out front and gets a pass from (3). (4) may now:

a. pass to (1) who is coming back to the ball off a screen by (3) as in Diagram 2-21.

b. work a screen-and-roll with (5) as in Diagram 2-22.

THE SCREEN-AWAY PLAY

(1) passes to (3), makes his outside cut, and (3) returns the ball to him. Then (3) moves away to screen for the offside guard. High-post man, (5), hesitates, then joins (3) in the double screen. The offside guard, (2), cuts to the basket and, if he isn't open, swings around the offside forward, (4). See Diagram 2-23.

(3) then does a reverse pivot and attempts to rub his man off on (5) as he cuts to the ballside lay-up area in Diagram 2-24.

If (3) is not open, (5) steps to the head of the key and (1) passes to him. (1) then screens down for (3), and (2) loops around (4). (5) passes to the open man. See Diagram 2-25.

FORWARD FAKE STACK PLAY

Many teams attempt to disallow the return pass from (3) to (1) that keys the play. When this happens, the forward fake stack play may be run. Forward, (3), keeps the ball and (1) continues around him to the ballside low-post area. See Diagram 2-26.

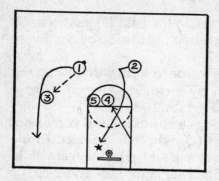

Diagram 2-20

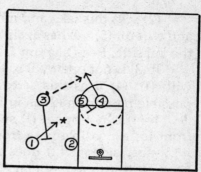

Diagram 2-21

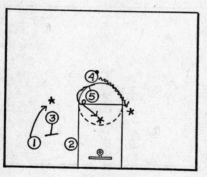

Diagram 2-22

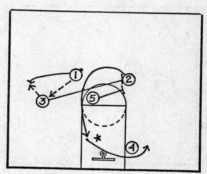

Diagram 2-23

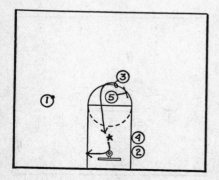

Diagram 2-24

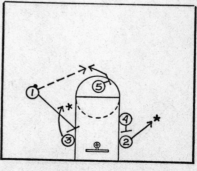

Diagram 2-25

(2) sees this fake and moves to the ball. (3) passes to (2) and cuts off (5). (4) has again cleared the offside by coming to the ballside. See Diagram 2-27.

If (3) is not open, (5) rolls inside to form a double screen with (1). (4) uses this screen by swinging around it for a possible pass from (2) as in Diagram 2-28.

If (4) is not open, (1) swings around (3) and comes out front for a possible pass from (2), who has dribbled to the high-post side. If (2) does not pass to (1), the team is in position to run a new play. See Diagrams 2-29 and 2-30.

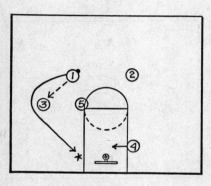

Diagram 2-26

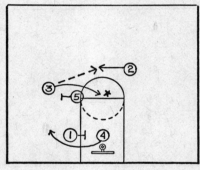

Diagram 2-27

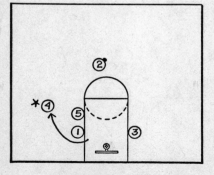

Diagram 2-28

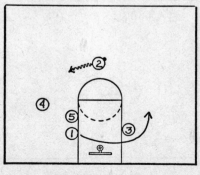

Diagram 2-29

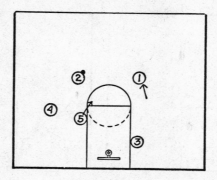

Diagram 2-30

THE FORWARD FAKE GUARD-AROUND PLAY

Guard, (1), passes to his forward, (3), and makes an outside cut and does not get the return pass. This tells the offside guard, (2), to cut over the post man to the ballside low post and then across the lane to form a natural screen for the offside forward, (4). See Diagram 2-31.

(4) then uses (2)'s cut and moves to the ballside low-post area for a possible pass from (3) as seen in Diagram 2-32.

If (4) is not open, high-post man, (5), screens down and away for (2), who continues around for a possible jump shot at the free throw line. See Diagram 2-33.

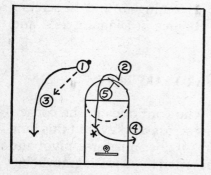

Diagram 2-31

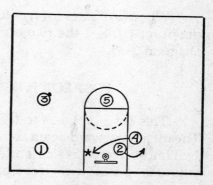

Diagram 2-32

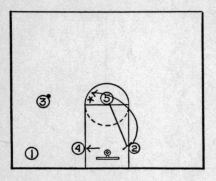

Diagram 2-33

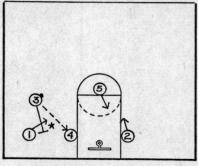

Diagram 2-34

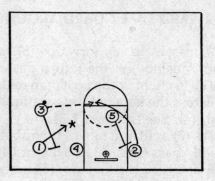

Diagram 2-35

When (3) passes to (4) or to (2) coming around, he screens down for (1). See the two possibilities in Diagram 2-34 and Diagram 2-35.

POST LOB FORWARD FAKE PLAY

This time (3) fakes to (1), who continues to the corner. The offside forward again comes across the key, but this time he blind-screens (5)'s defender. (5) does a reverse pivot and cuts to the basket to receive a pass from (3). See Diagram 2-36.

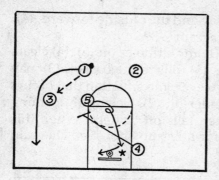

Diagram 2-36

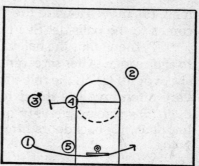

Diagram 2-37

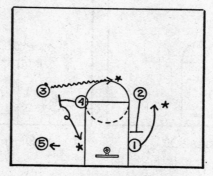

Diagram 2-38

If (5) isn't open, (1) continues around to the opposite side and (5) cuts to the ballside low-post area. See Diagram 2-37.

(3) then dribbles off (4) and the basic options prevail, which are shown in Diagram 2-38.

FORWARD FAKE AND DRIBBLE PLAY

This play works very well when used in conjunction with the forward lob play. It begins as guard, (1), passes to his forward, (3) and makes an outside cut. At the same time, post man, (5), moves toward the play and the outside forward, (4), comes to the ballside. See Diagram 2-39.

(3) then fakes the ball to (1) and dribbles off (5). (4) clears to the corner. After screening, (5) rolls to the basket. (3) may shoot or hit (5) on the roll. However, the situation that occurs very often involves the defender on (2). Seeing (3) coming over (5)'s screen, he very often falls off to help. When this happens, (2) backdoors him for a lay-up shot. See Diagram 2-40.

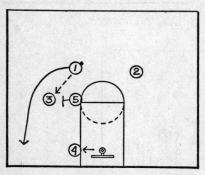
Diagram 2-39

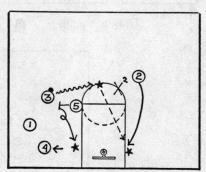
Diagram 2-40

FORWARD FAKE-TO-FLEX CONTINUITY PLAY

Guard, (1), passes to forward, (3), and makes an outside cut. (3) fakes the ball to (1) and (1) continues to the ballside corner. This tells the offside guard, (2), to cut off the high-post man to the ballside low-post area. See Diagram 2-41.

At this point, (4)'s defender will often drop off to help on cutter, (2). To take advantage of this, the post man, (5), screens away for (4), who cuts to the high-post area. See Diagram 2-42.

As soon as (3) passes to (4), (2) steps out and screens for (1), who cuts to the basket and then across the lane. See Diagram 2-43 for this maneuver. (3) then down screens for (2), who pops out for a possible pass from (4). See Diagram 2-44.

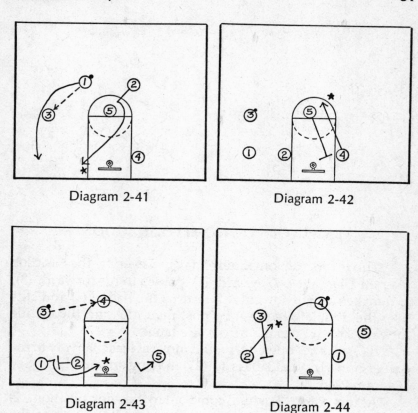

Diagram 2-41

Diagram 2-42

Diagram 2-43

Diagram 2-44

Forward Fake-to-Double-Down Option

(1) passes to (3), makes an outside cut, and (3) fakes to him. (1) continues his cut to the ballside corner. (2) then slashes off (5) and to the ballside low-post area. See Diagram 2-45.

The sequence continues as (5) screens away for (4), who moves to the head of the key. (3) passes to (4) as (3) and (1) screen down for (2), who pops out to the wing. (4)'s options are to shoot, look for (2) coming off the double screen, or pass to (5) in the low-post area for a one-on-one play. See Diagram 2-46.

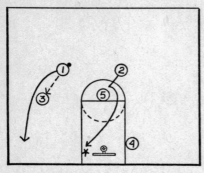 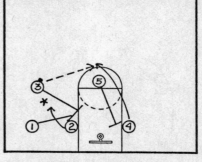

Diagram 2-45   Diagram 2-46

BASIC LOB PLAY-TO-REVERSE ACTION

The reverse action pattern may be keyed by the basic lob play. In Diagram 2-47, guard, (1), passes to his forward, (3), and makes an outside cut. (3) returns the ball to (1) and cuts over the double screen set by post man, (5), and the offside forward, (4), who came across the lane.

If (3) was not open, (4) would move at least halfway to the corner and (1) would pass to (2), moving toward him. See Diagram 2-48.

At this point, (3) would come out to the wing position. (2) would pass to him, make a cut outside and continue to the corner. The team would then be in pattern set to run the reverse action pattern. See Diagrams 2-49 and 2-50.

The lob play may also be interjected into the reverse action pattern. At the point the front man passes to the wing man and cuts outside, the lob play may be keyed by the wing man returning the ball to the outside cutter. Using the pattern in action numbers shown in Diagram 2-50, (5) returns the ball to (4) and cuts over (3). This signals (1) to come across the lane. See Diagram 2-51.

If (5) was not open, (1) could move halfway to the corner. (4) would pass to (2) as in Diagram 2-52. From there, the reverse action pattern may again be run.

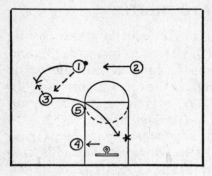

Diagram 2-47

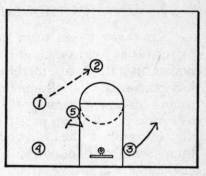

Diagram 2-48

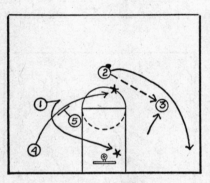

Diagram 2-49

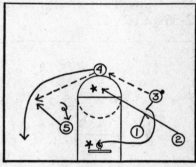

Diagram 2-50

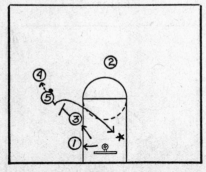

Diagram 2-51

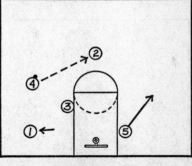

Diagram 2-52

OUTSIDE CUT TO SHUFFLE

One way to get from the outside cut key to a shuffle offense is as follows: Guard, (1), passes to forward, (3), and makes his outside cut. (3) returns the ball to (1) and cuts to the low-post area. At the same time, on the offside, forward, (4), moves up and screens for (2), who cuts to the offside lay-up slot for a possible lob pass from (1). See Diagram 2-53.

(4) breaks to the head of the key to take a pass from (1). (4) then passes to (2), moving out to the wing area. This tells (1) to cut low, off the double screen by (5) and (3). See Diagram 2-54.

After (1) has cut, (5) swings to the ballside and (4) screens for (3), who moves to the head of the key. Garland Pinholster's Pinwheel Shuffle is now in operation. See Diagrams 2-55 and 2-56.

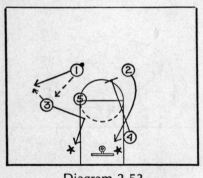

Diagram 2-53

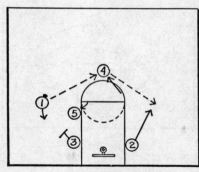

Diagram 2-54

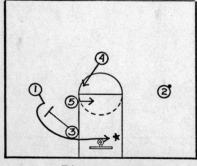

Diagram 2-55

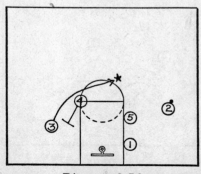

Diagram 2-56

3

DRIBBLE ENTRY
PLAYS

The dribble entry play is very valuable to a team that must face strong defensive pressure. It allows the ball to be advanced to the forward position without the necessity of a pass. Getting the ball to the forward position is strategically important because it facilitates a quick pass to the low post, high post, or to the head of the key.

Another advantage of the dribble entry key is that it is adaptable to a great many plays. In most other plays, the ball is passed to the forward position and then a cut is made by the passer. On dribble entry plays, the ball is dribbled to the forward position and the forward in that position must vacate and cut somewhere. Because of these similarities, many of the inside cut plays mentioned in Chapter One may be run from a dribble entry key.

BASIC UCLA PLAY

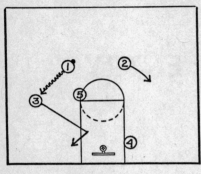

Diagram 3-1

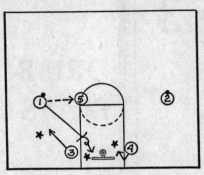

Diagram 3-2

POST EXCHANGE CONTINUITY

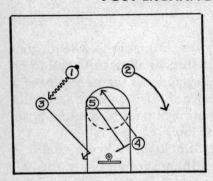

Diagram 3-3

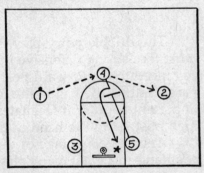

Diagram 3-4

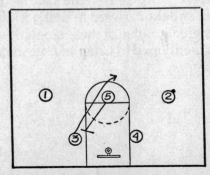

Diagram 3-5

WEAK SIDE

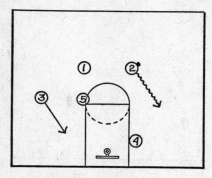

Diagram 3-6

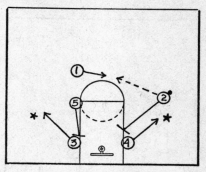

Diagram 3-7

REVERSE OR SPLIT

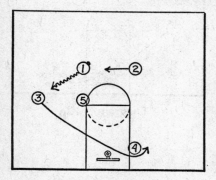

Diagram 3-8

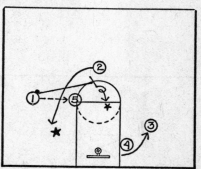

Diagram 3-9

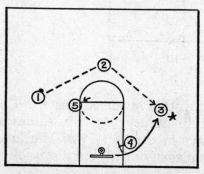

Diagram 3-10

TRIANGLE PLAY

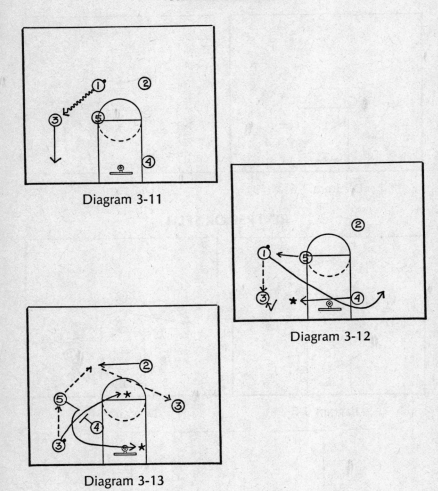

Diagram 3-11

Diagram 3-12

Diagram 3-13

Many of the other inside cut plays in Chapter One may also be run as dribble entry plays. The same idea applies to the outside cut plays in Chapter Two. The following few diagrams are examples of outside cut plays converted to dribble entry plays.

FORWARD LOB PLAY

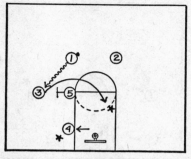

Diagram 3-14

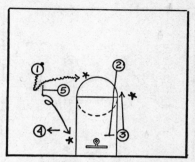

Diagram 3-15

SCREEN-AWAY PLAY

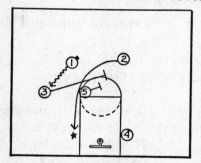

Diagram 3-16

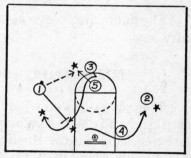

Diagram 3-17

LOW-POST ISOLATION PLAY

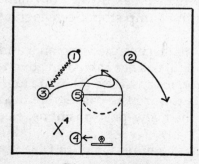

Diagram 3-18

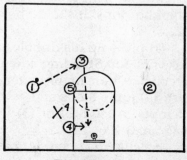

Diagram 3-19

THE OFFSIDE LOB PLAY

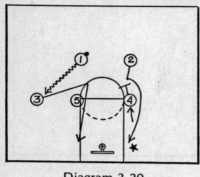

Diagram 3-20

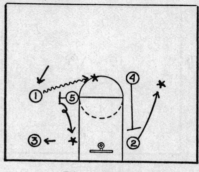

Diagram 3-21

The following plays also may be run from the dribble entry key.

DRIBBLE ENTRY HIGH-POST FEED PLAY

This play is keyed when guard, (1), dribbles toward forward, (3), and clears him across the lane to the offside low-post area. This tells the offside guard, (2), to fan to the far wing area; the high-post man, (5), to drop to the ballside low-post area; and the offside forward, (4), to break sharply to the high-post area. (4)'s move is particularly important. He must get close to his opponent and then break away from him. When he stops, it should be with a jump stop. See Diagram 3-22.

(1) picks up his dribble as he reaches the wing area and looks first for (5) sliding down. If (5) has not gained an advantageous position on his defender, (3) passes to (4) in the high post. (4) jump stops and pivots toward the basket. He then attempts to feed (5) or (3) in their low-post positions. See Diagram 3-23.

If neither is open, (4) passes to either wing. In Diagram

3-24, he passes to wingman, (2). Upon receiving the ball, (2) looks first for (3), the man in the low-post area. This option is often open because (3)'s defender was probably overplaying him toward the ball when (4) was attempting to feed him. (3) can exploit being open by moving toward X3 as the pass is made from (4) to (2). He then pivots toward the basket and this pins X3 out of position.

If (3) is not open, (2) looks for (1), breaking to the head of the key off a double screen by (4) and (5). See Diagram 3-25.

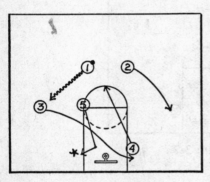

Diagram 3-22

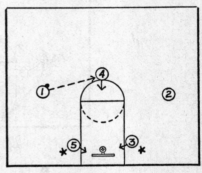

Diagram 3-23

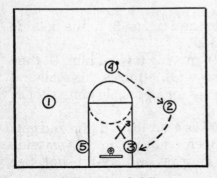

Diagram 3-24

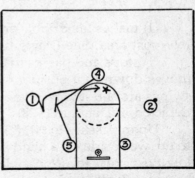

Diagram 3-25

Special Lay-Up Option

At the point where (1) breaks off the double screen, a special option may be run. This is keyed by (3) who, instead of posting, moves out as if to screen for (2). This clears the area under the basket and gives (1) room to cut low for a possible lay-up. Since (3), who is coming out, congests the ballside it is advisable for (2) to use a two-hand overhead pass to (1). See Diagram 3-26.

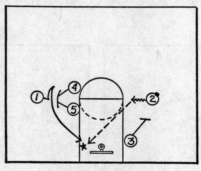

Diagram 3-26

THE WALL PLAY

(1) makes his dribble entry and clears (3) to the ballside low-post area. See Diagram 3-27.

(1) stops and passes to (2), moving toward him. (1) then moves down to a position above (3). (4) uses this wall and swings around it to receive a pass for a possible jump shot as depicted in Diagram 3-28.

Upon passing to (4), (2) fakes a cut toward him and cuts to the weak side off a blind screen set by (5), to the weakside low-post area, for a possible lob pass and lay-up shot. See Diagram 3-29.

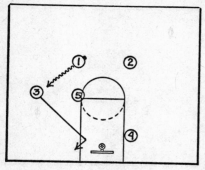

Diagram 3-27

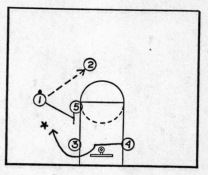

Diagram 3-28

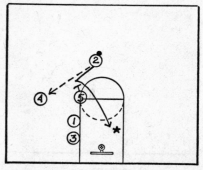

Diagram 3-29

WEAKSIDE STACK PLAY

(1) cannot get the ball to his forward, (3), so he dribbles at guard, (2). This tells (2) to down screen for forward, (4). (4) uses the screen and cuts diagonally to the wing area. See Diagram 3-30.

(1) passes to (4). As this pass is made, (3) cuts off (5) on the weak side and moves to the ballside high-post area. After screening, (5) rolls to the offside low-post area for a possible lob pass. See Diagram 3-31.

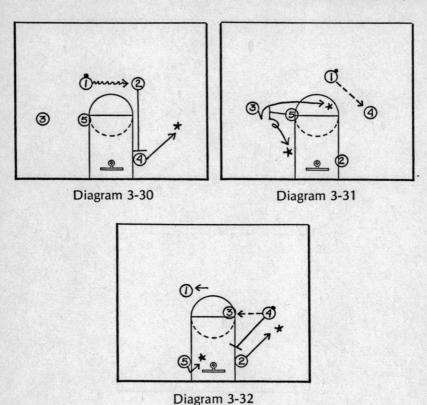

Diagram 3-30   Diagram 3-31

Diagram 3-32

(4) then passes to (3) and screens down for (2). (3) may shoot, pass to (2), who is coming out, or look for (4) or (5) inside. (1) moves away to keep his defender from jamming in on (3). See Diagram 3-32.

DIAGONAL DRIBBLE ENTRY PLAY

To key this play, the offside guard, (2), clears over the top of the post to the far low-post area. This tells the offside forward, (4), to clear across the lane and the guard with the ball, (1), to dribble off high-post man, (5). (1) penetrates as far as he can. See Diagram 3-33.

As soon as (1) picks up his dribble, forward, (3), cuts low off the double screen set by (2) and (4). See Diagram 3-34.

If (3) is not open, (5) steps out to the head of the key and (1) passes to him. (4) then pops out diagonally and (1) screens down for (3), who also pops out. See Diagram 3-35.

DRIBBLE ENTRY POWER SERIES

The play is started by the guard without the ball. In Diagram 3-36 the guard, (2), clears down and around high-post man, (5). Guard, (1), dribbles off (5) to penetrate and look for a possible jump shot or a pass to (4) in the low-post area. From there, many options may occur.

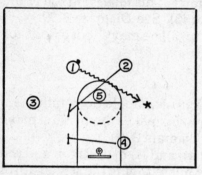

Diagram 3-33

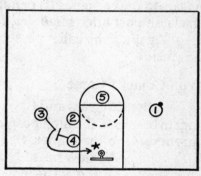

Diagram 3-34

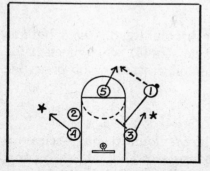

Diagram 3-35

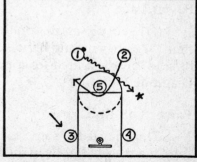

Diagram 3-36

Post Exchange

Post man, (5), comes down and screens for the offside forward, (3). This temporarily takes away the offside defensive help. (3) breaks to the ballside. If (1) passes to (3), he may shoot or look for (4) inside the defender who fronted him to prevent the pass from (1). See Diagram 3-37.

Power Split

(1) may pass to (4) and split the post with (3) as illustrated in Diagram 3-38.

The Power Roll

This option is keyed when (4) yells "clear" and then clears to the corner as (1) penetrates. This tells (5) to roll to the ballside post after screening for (3). See Diagram 3-39.

Again, if the ball is passed to (3), he may shoot or look for (5) inside.

You Come, I Come

After (2) clears and (1) makes his dribble penetration, (3) again breaks to the high post, and (5) makes the clearing move around (4) to the corner. See Diagram 3-40.

The ball is now passed to (4), and (1) may screen and roll with either (3) or (5). The player not receiving the screen [(3) or (5)] will backdoor his defender. See Diagrams 3-41 and 3-42.

Power Lob

(1) again penetrates on the dribble after (2) clears, but this time (3) comes up and blind screens for (5), who wheels to the offside low-post area for a possible crosscourt lob pass. See Diagram 3-43.

Power Lob Roll

This play is the same as the previous one but (4) clears to the corner and (3) rolls to the ballside low-post after screening for (5). (3) looks for a pass from (1). See Diagram 3-44.

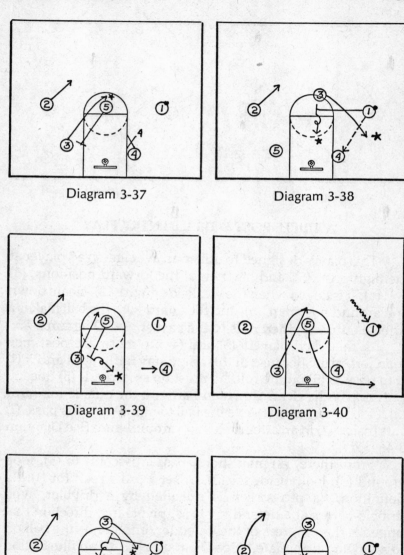

Diagram 3-37

Diagram 3-38

Diagram 3-39

Diagram 3-40

Diagram 3-41

Diagram 3-42

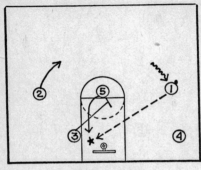 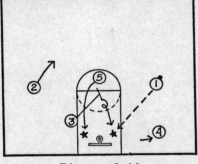

Diagram 3-43   Diagram 3-44

A TRIPLE-POST DRIBBLE ENTRY PLAY

This play is designed to utilize an average-sized player at the high post, (5), and big men at the forward positions, (3) and (4). It is keyed when the weakside guard, (2), clears down and around post man, (5), and the guard with the ball makes a dribble entry. (5) then rolls to the basket. See Diagram 3-45.

In this play, players (3) and (4) are more like post men than forwards. Because of this, they stay fairly tight and if (1) is to pass to (5) on the roll, he must do so early. If (5) doesn't get the pass he clears down and around the offside forward, (3). (4) posts up and (1) gets the ball to him. After this pass, (1) cuts inside (4) in an attempt to loop around him. See Diagram 3-46.

From there, (4) may shoot, pass crosscourt to (5), loop around (3), look inside for (3), or set a pro screen for (1). By definition, "a pro screen is executed by a dribbler, who dribble-drives at a defender, stops, pivots in a direction that impedes the progress of the defender, and hands the ball off to a moving teammate." See Diagram 3-47 for an illustration of this technique.

Another workable option is presented after (4) has exhausted all the other options. (3) steps out and screens for (5), who goes baseline and takes a pass from (4) for a lay-up. See Diagram 3-48.

(2) is the back man who maintains defensive balance. He is also the safety valve man who calls for the ball and resets the play when things get scrambled. See Diagram 3-49.

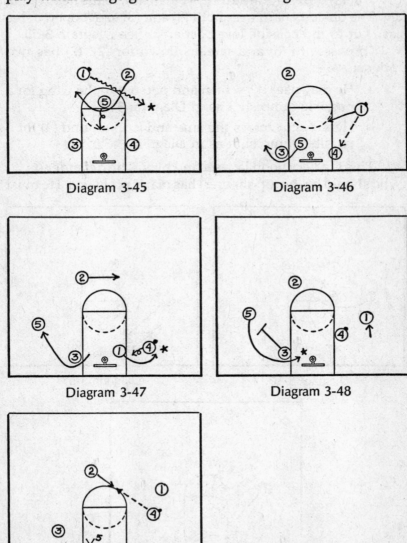

Diagram 3-45

Diagram 3-46

Diagram 3-47

Diagram 3-48

Diagram 3-49

HIGH CLEAR SLASH PLAY

The high clear slash play begins as (1) dribbles at his forward, (3). (3) clears around post man, (5), to the head of the key. The offside guard uses both (3) and (5) to get open in his slash cut to the ballside low-post area. See Diagram 3-50.

(1) passes to (3) and screens down for (2). (2) has two options:

    a. He may use (1)'s screen and pop out to the wing for a possible jump shot as in Diagram 3-51.

    b. He may cut across the lane and loop around (4) for a possible jump shot as in Diagram 3-52.

This is a very good last-second play. The defender on (2) (who should be the top shooter) has many problems. He must

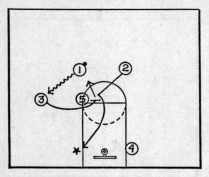

Diagram 3-50

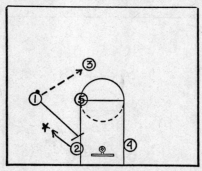

Diagram 3-51

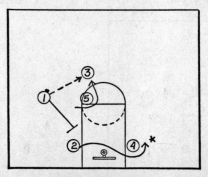

Diagram 3-52

first get over a double screen, then beat (2) around the screen he chooses to utilize.

HIGH CLEAR POST-DOWN PLAY

As (1) makes his dribble entry, the offside guard, (2), fans to the far wing area and the onside forward, (3), swings down and around post man, (5), and to the point. This cut acts as a natural screen for (5), and he slides down to the low-post area. See Diagram 3-53.

(1) looks first for (5) in the low post and then passes to (3) at the point. After this pass, (5) clears down and around (4), and (2) cuts over (4). See Diagram 3-54.

If neither (2) nor (5) are open, (3) dribbles toward (1)'s side and (1) screens down for (2) who pops out for a possible jump shot. See Diagram 3-55.

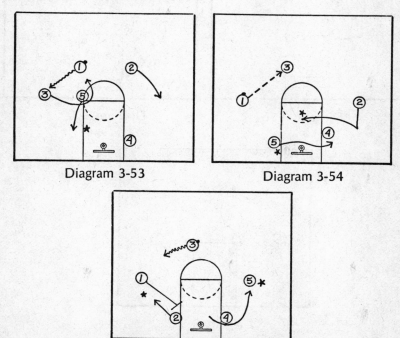

Diagram 3-53

Diagram 3-54

Diagram 3-55

ISOLATION PLAYS

High Clear Isolation Play

(1) again dribbles at (3) and clears him to the head of the key. (4) swings across the lane to the ballside and (2) fans to the offside wing. See Diagram 3-56.

(1) attempts to get the ball to (4), who will probably be fronted. If (1) cannot get the ball to (4), he swings it to (3) and the reversal continues to (2) in an attempt to catch (4)'s defender out of position. See Diagram 3-57 and Diagram 3-58.

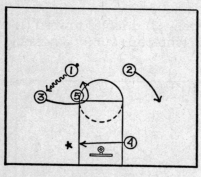

Diagram 3-56

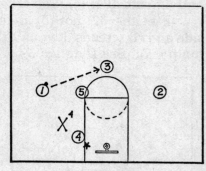

Diagram 3-57

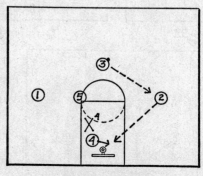

Diagram 3-58

Low-Post Clear Isolation Play

As (1) makes his dribble entry, (3) clears to the ballside low-post area. At the same time, (4) comes across the lane and continues to the ballside corner. See Diagram 3-59.

Note in Diagram 3-59 that (2) cleared away and (5) stepped out. These moves cleared the entire post area for (3). The men on the perimeter then attempt to get the ball to (3).

Corner Clear Isolation Play

This time as (1) makes his dribble entry, the ballside forward clears to the corner, the post man swings low, the offside guard, (2), clears away, and the offside forward, (4), cuts to the head of the key. The perimeter men then attempt to get the ball to (5). See Diagram 3-60.

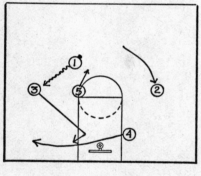

Diagram 3-59

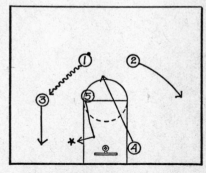

Diagram 3-60

4

PLAYS KEYED BY A GUARD-TO-GUARD PASS

Guard-to-guard passes are becoming more important because the pressure-and-help man-to-man defense has made penetration passes (guard-to-forward or guard-to-post man) very difficult. Following are some plays that are keyed by a guard-to-guard pass.

THE LOB-AND-SCREEN-AWAY PLAY

This play begins as guard, (1), passes to guard, (2), and cuts off high-post man, (5), for a possible lob pass. The possibility of this pass succeeding is greatly enhanced by the position of the forwards. When (1) had the ball, he caused (3) to play as high as the free throw line extended. When (1) passed to (2), it brought (4) as high as the free throw line extended on his side of the court. Thus, during the time of the lob pass, both forwards and their defenders had cleared the free throw lane area. See Diagram 4-1.

If (1) is not open, (2) dribbles at forward, (3), and passes to him. By then, (1) has crossed the lane and is in position to screen for (4). (4) uses this screen and cuts low and across the lane. This is shown in Diagram 4-2.

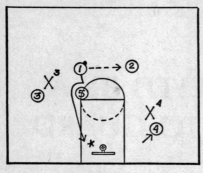

Diagram 4-1

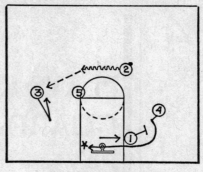

Diagram 4-2

From there, the coach may teach the offense in either of two ways:

A. *Twice Around*

Positioning the players as they are in Diagram 4-2, (2) screens opposite for (1), and (1) comes to the point as in Diagram 4-3.

(3) reverses the ball to (2) by way of (1) and cuts off (4) as in Diagram 4-4.

If (3) was not open, (2) dribbles out front, and a new play would be run. See Diagram 4-5.

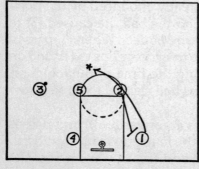

Diagram 4-3

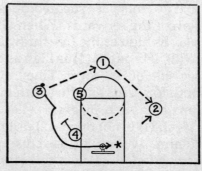

Diagram 4-4

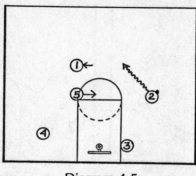

Diagram 4-5

B. Continuity

Again, positioning the players as they were at the conclusion of Diagram 4-4, (2) screens opposite for (1), who cuts to the point. The ball is reversed to (2) by way of (1). But this time, after (1) passes to (2), he screens opposite for (4), who comes to the point. Diagrams 4-6 through 4-9 show the continuity in action.

During this continuity, if the ball is thrown to the post man, (5) (who always cuts to the ballside), the passer, (4), screens down for the low cutter, (1). See Diagram 4-10.

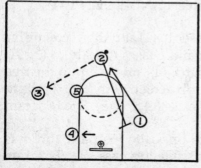

Diagram 4-6

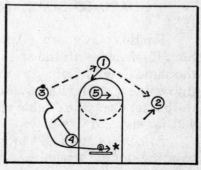

Diagram 4-7

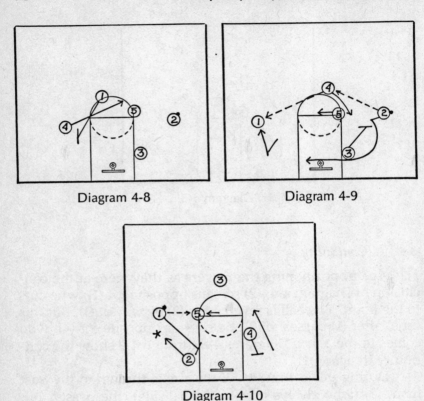

Diagram 4-8   Diagram 4-9

Diagram 4-10

GUARD-TO-GUARD SCREEN-AND-ROLL PLAY

For this play guard, (1), passes to (2) and then screens for him. (2) dribbles off the screen and passes quickly to (3). At the same time, the offside forward, (4), moves up to the free throw line area and forms a double screen with (5). (1) rolls to the basket using the double screen of (4) and (5). See Diagram 4-11 for steps in this play.

In continuation, (2) moves opposite his pass and cuts over the double screen for a possible lob pass. See Diagram 4-12.

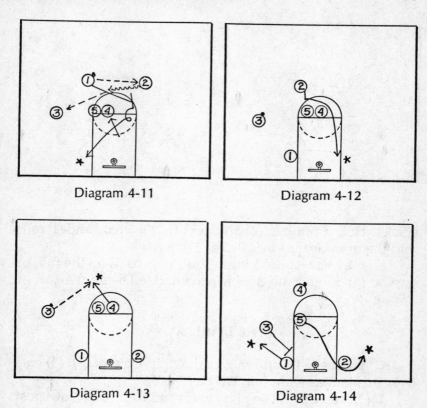

Diagram 4-11

Diagram 4-12

Diagram 4-13

Diagram 4-14

If neither (1) nor (2) get open on their initial cuts, (4) steps to the point using (5) to rub his man off and receives a pass from (3). See Diagram 4-13.

(3) then screens down for (2) and (5) loops down and around (2). (4) feeds the double stack. See Diagram 4-14.

THE SCREEN-AND-ROLL CLEAR PLAY

The guard, (1), on the side of the stack created by (5) and (3) passes to the other guard, (2), and moves across to screen for him. This tells the forward, (4), across the lane from the

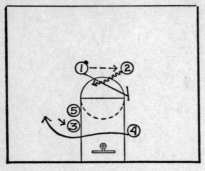

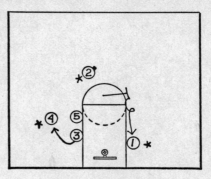

Diagram 4-15   Diagram 4-16

stack to clear around it. (2) dribbles off (1)'s screen and (1) rolls into the area cleared by (4). See Diagram 4-15.

(2) may now shoot a jump shot, pass to (1) on the roll, or pass to (4) behind the double screen. See Diagram 4-16.

THE JAM PLAY

(1) passes to (2) and moves down in front of (5). (3) cuts over this jam as shown in Diagram 4-17.

If (3) isn't open, (1) spins off (5) and rolls to the low-post area looking for a pass from (2). (5) moves to the front. At times, he may be open because his man may hedge or switch on (3) or (1). See Diagram 4-18.

After (2) passes to (5) he loops down and around (1). At the same time (4) screens down for (3). (5) feeds the double stack. See Diagram 4-19.

LAST-SECOND GAME WINNER PLAY

The idea of this play is to get a last-second shot for your best player, (4). This is done by having guard, (2), pass to (1) and screen down for (4) in the low-post area. At the same

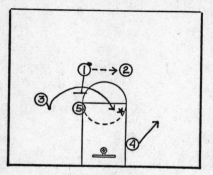

Diagram 4-17

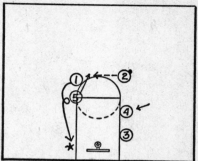

Diagram 4-18

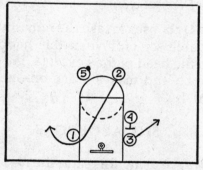

Diagram 4-19

time, the forward, (3), moves in close to form a vertical double screen with the post man, (5). (4) now has two options:

A. Use the Single Screen

(4) simply moves out front off (2)'s screen. Note that after screening for (4) and seeing him move out front, (2) cleared around (3) and (5)'s double screen. See Diagrams 4-20 and 4-21.

(2)'s clearing move around the double screen gives (4) room to work and gives (1) another option in case (4) cannot get open.

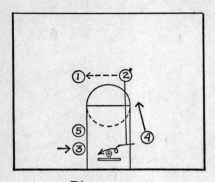

Diagram 4-20

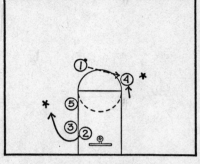

Diagram 4-21

B. *Use the Double Screen*

This time (4) chooses to fake the move out front and cuts around the double screen. When this happens, (2) moves quickly back to the head of the key. If (4) is open, (2) again is the second option and makes a one-on-one play. See Diagrams 4-22 and 4-23.

SPECIAL OPTIONS

Another way of using this same idea is to place (4) in the post. Then, the guard (1)-to-guard (2) pass is made and (1) screens down for (4). At that point three options may occur:

    a. (4) may use (1)'s screen and move out front. See Diagram 4-24.

    b. (4) may fake the cut out front and loop around (5) after moving across the lane. See Diagram 4-25.

    c. (4) may fake the cut out front and cut to the offside low-post area. (5) has vacated this area and received a pass from (2). (4) then makes a one-on-one low-post play. See Diagram 4-26.

In all three options (3) moves out to provide defensive balance and the other four men crash the boards.

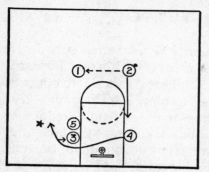

Diagram 4-22

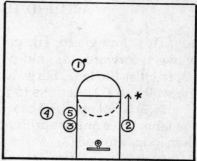

Diagram 4-23

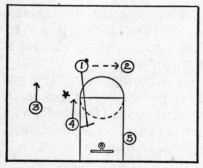

Diagram 4-24

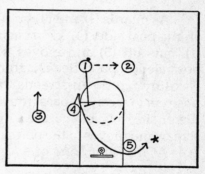

Diagram 4-25

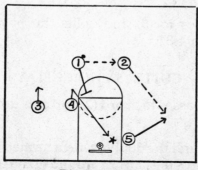

Diagram 4-26

AROUND THE STACK PLAY

This time guard, (1), passes to (2) and then cuts down between forward, (3), and post man, (5). This tells forward, (4), to cross the lane. Forward, (3), uses (1) and (5) to cut over the wall and (2) attempts to pass to him. See Diagram 4-27.

If (3) is not open, he continues to the low-post area across the lane. (1) continues around the stack, across the lane, and then loops around (3). At the same time post man, (5), screens down for (4) and (2) feeds the double stack. See Diagram 4-28.

GUARD LOB PLAY

As guards (1) and (2) bring the ball up court, the forward on the post side, (4), clears across the lane. (2) then passes to (1), cuts off (5) and moves to the offside lay-up slot for a possible lob pass. See Diagram 4-29.

(3) then down screens for (4), who moves to the wing position to receive a pass from (1). (1) passes to (4) and clears to the offside low-post area. At the same time, (2) uses (5) as a screen and moves to the point area as Diagram 4-30 illustrates.

At this time, one of two options may occur:

a. (4) may pass to (2) at the point and screen down for (3). At the same time, (5) screens down for (1). (3) and (1) cut to their respective wing positions. See Diagram 4-31.

b. (4) passes to (3) and splits the post with (2). See Diagram 4-32.

CUTTER'S CHOICE PLAY

Guard (1) passes to guard (2) and cuts down the lane. He may now:

a. Cut around the double screen formed by (5) and (3) on one side of the lane, or around (4) on the other side. In

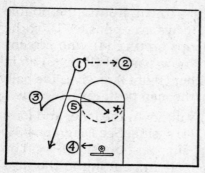

Diagram 4-27

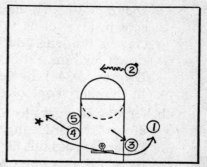

Diagram 4-28

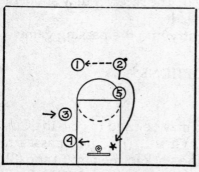

Diagram 4-29

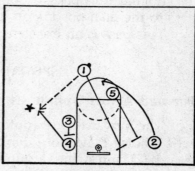

Diagram 4-30

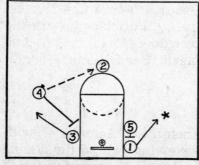

Diagram 4-31

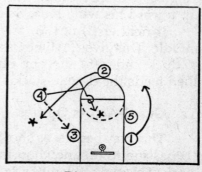

Diagram 4-32

Diagram 4-33, (1) chooses to cut around the double screen. (3)'s job is to always go opposite (1), so he crosses the lane and loops around (4) who screens down for him. (2) may now pass to (1) or (3) as in Diagram 4-34. When either (1) or (3) receives the ball, he may shoot or look to the man posting on his side.

b. (1) may also pass to (2), cut down the lane, and loop around the single man, (4)'s, side. See Diagram 4-35. When he does this (3) again goes opposite (1)'s cut by using (5) as a down screen and cutting to the near wing position as in Diagram 4-36.

(2) may now pass to (3) or (1). The receiver may shoot or pass to the man posting on his side.

This pass is an excellent entry into the passing game.

SPECIAL OPTIONS

Forward-Across Option

The forward-across option may be used to give the Cutter's Choice Play more depth. Guard, (1), again passes to guard, (2), and swings around the stack formed by (5) and (3). This time, however, (3) moves up and around (5)'s down screen and swings across the lane looking for a pass from (2). To give (3) more room in which to work, forward, (4), moves up toward his wing area. See Diagrams 4-37 and 4-38.

If neither (1) nor (3) are open, (2) dribbles toward the middle. This gives (4) time to screen down for (3), and (1) time to duck under (5) and pop out again. See Diagram 4-39. (2) then feeds the double stack.

The Guard-Across Option

This play begins, as shown before in Diagram 4-37, with (1) passing to (2) and choosing to swing around the double stack. This time, the guard goes all the way around the stack

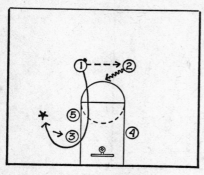

Diagram 4-33

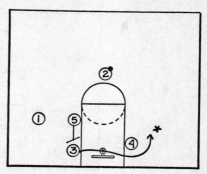

Diagram 4-34

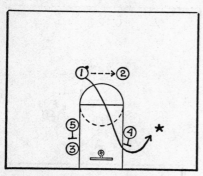

Diagram 4-35

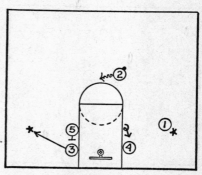

Diagram 4-36

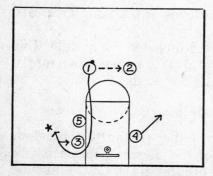

Diagram 4-37

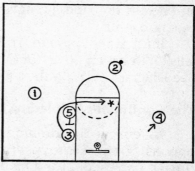

Diagram 4-38

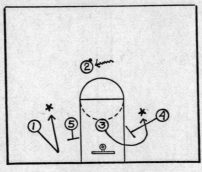

Diagram 4-39

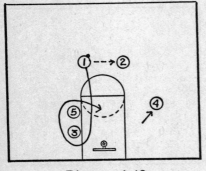

Diagram 4-40

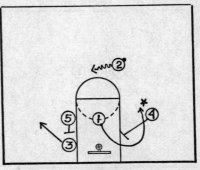

Diagram 4-41

and across the lane. (4) again moves to the wing area. See Diagram 4-40.

If (2) cannot pass to (1), he dribbles to the middle. This tells (5) to screen down for (3), and (4) to screen down for (1). See Diagram 4-41. (2) then feeds the double stack.

The Continuous Triple Stack Option

If, during the running of either of the two previous options, (2) chooses to pass to (4), the following option may be run. (1) passes to (2) and loops around the stack. (3) runs the

Forward-Across Option by moving across the lane. Neither (1) nor (3) is open, so (2) passes to (4) and cuts by him, providing a screen that allows him to dribble to the point. See Diagram 4-42.

This tells (1) to move inside of (5), and (3) to loop around them as Diagram 4-43 illustrates.

From there, either the Forward-Across or Guard-Across Option could be run. See Diagrams 4-44 and 4-45.

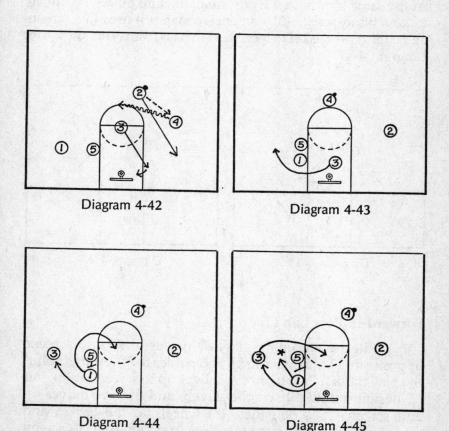

Diagram 4-42

Diagram 4-43

Diagram 4-44

Diagram 4-45

GUARD-TO-GUARD LOB SERIES

Forward-to-Forward Lob Play

This play is keyed when guard, (1), passes to guard, (2), and screens opposite for (3), who comes to the front. Post man, (5), swings to the ballside. See Diagram 4-46.

(4) then moves up to be in position to receive a pass from (2) and to clear the lane area. (2) fakes a pass to (3), which causes (3)'s defender to play him tightly. (2) then passes to (4). At the same time both the post man, (5), and guard, (1), move up and blind-screen (3)'s defensive man. (3) uses this screen and cuts to the basket to receive a lob pass from (4) as shown in Diagram 4-47.

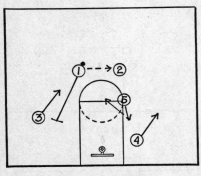

Diagram 4-46

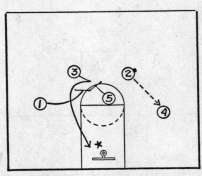

Diagram 4-47

Forward-to-Post Lob Play

As in the preceding play, (1) passes to (2) and screens opposite for (3). (2) fakes to (3) and passes to (4). At this point, the play differs. Post man, (5), moves up to screen for (3), but (2) hesitates until (5) sets the screen, and then he moves up and screens (5)'s defender. (5) wheels to the basket and receives the lob pass from (4). Note that to make (5)'s screen look authentic, (3) fanned to his wing area. See Diagram 4-48.

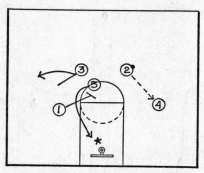

Diagram 4-48

A Two-Option Pressure-Relieving Play

Guard (1) in Diagram 4-49 is unable to make a penetration pass so he passes to guard, (2). This tells post man, (5), to step out and screen for forward, (3), who cuts low off him to the low-post area. From there, one of two options may be run:

A. Guard Lob Option

In this option, (5), after screening for (3), would move up and screen for guard, (1), who cuts to the basket for a possible lob pass. See Diagram 4-50.

The offside forward, (4), would then pinch in and, with (3), form a double screen. (1) loops around the wall. See Diagram 4-51.

If (1) is not open, (2) could work a screen-and-roll play with (5). See Diagram 4-52.

B. Screen Away Option

In this option, (1) crosses in front of (2) in his cut, to form a double screen with (3). (5) then steps up and (2) penetrates as far as he can on the dribble. See Diagram 4-53.

Once (2) has been stopped and can't shoot, (4) cuts to the ballside off the double screen of (1) and (3). To facilitate this cut, (5) didn't roll after screening for (2). See Diagram 4-54.

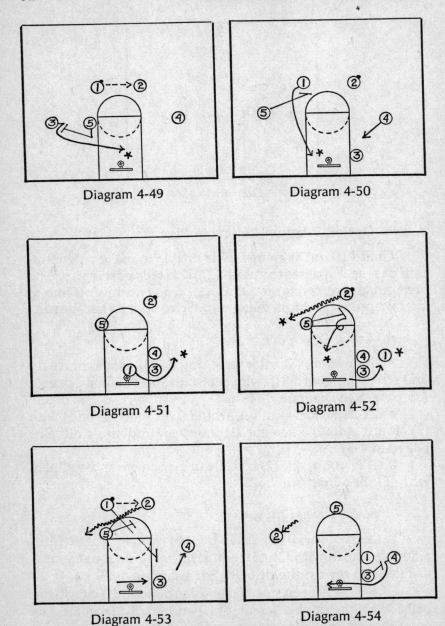

Diagram 4-49

Diagram 4-50

Diagram 4-51

Diagram 4-52

Diagram 4-53

Diagram 4-54

Guard-to-Guard-to-Pivot Rotation Play

This play begins as guard, (1), passes to guard, (2), and then cuts over a screen set by forward, (3). (3) slides out to the free throw line extended area. See Diagram 4-55.

(2) looks first for a lob pass to (1). If (1) is not open, (5) cuts across the free throw lane, as (1) loops around (4) as in Diagram 4-56.

(2) looks first for (5) and then may pass to either wing area. In Diagram 4-57, he chooses to pass to (1), who looped around (4) and moved to the wing area on that side. This tells the onside post man, (4), that he must screen away for the offside post man, (5). (5) then moves to the ball.

Immediately after (4) screens for (5), (2) moves down the lane and screens for (4). (4) then cuts to the head of the key. See Diagram 4-58.

This move is a pivot rotation. If (2) had chosen to pass to (3), the rotation would have been as shown in Diagrams 4-59 and 4-60.

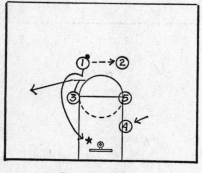

Diagram 4-55

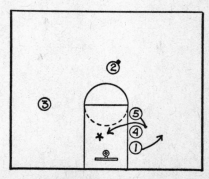

Diagram 4-56

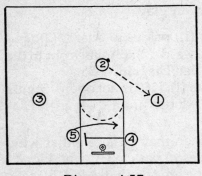

Diagram 4-57

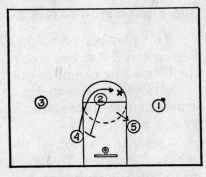

Diagram 4-58

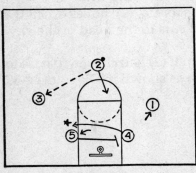

Diagram 4-59

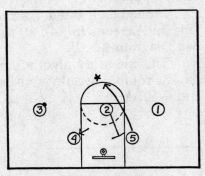

Diagram 4-60

5

PLAYS KEYED BY A PASS TO THE POST

The pass-to-the-post play has many functions. It may be used to take the defensive pressure off the onside forward, to feed the low-post positions, to engage the defensive post man, or to create a lot of movement by splitting the post. The following plays include a wide variety of maneuvers that will allow you to choose the one, or ones, that best fit your personnel.

THE SPLIT-CLEAR AND WALL PLAY

(1) passes to (5) and crosses in front of (2) on the way to forming a double screen (wall) with (4). The onside forward, (3), backdoors. (2) uses (1)'s cut as a natural screen and also cuts over (5) on his way to the area cleared by (3). See Diagram 5-1.

If neither (3) nor (2) are open, (3) continues across the lane and around the double screen of (1) and (4). (5) looks for (3) looping around the wall as shown in Diagram 5-2.

If (3) is not open, (2) breaks back to the ball and (5) passes to him. Then (3) breaks either high or low over the double screen and back to the ball. See Diagram 5-3.

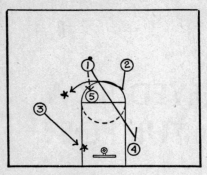

Diagram 5-1

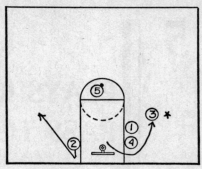

Diagram 5-2

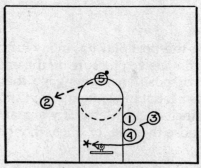

Diagram 5-3

SPREAD PLAY

This time, the spread play develops when (1) passes to
(5), and both he and (2) fan to their respective wing areas. (5)
holds the ball above his head and both (3) and (4) post up. See
Diagram 5-4.

(5) looks for the inside defender who is making the
strongest overplay. He then passes the ball to the guard on
that side of the floor. In Diagram 5-5, with X4 overplaying on

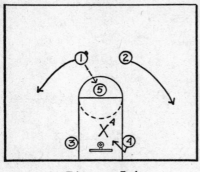

Diagram 5-4

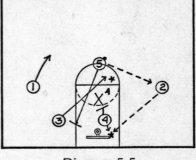

Diagram 5-5

defense, guard, (2), should have an excellent passing angle to (4) on the inside. It helps if (4) has the ability to pin his defender away from the ball.

Note that (5) and (3) exchanged to keep the help-side defenders busy.

Spread Play Post Exchange Option

A spread-type play may be initiated by a post exchange. In Diagram 5-6 post man, (5), screens for the offside forward, (4), who cuts to the high-post area. (1) passes to (4) and both guards, (1) and (2), fan to the wing area on their side of the court.

This key tells (3) to move across the lane and loop around (5). After his screening action, (5) cuts to the opposite low-post area. See Diagram 5-7.

This post exchange forces defensive adjustments. (4) could pass to (3) or (5) for a one-on-one play. If the defense denies these passes, (4) may pass to either wing [(1) or (2)], affording a better passing angle to one of the low-post areas. (4) then screens for the offside post man to take away the offside defensive help. See Diagram 5-8.

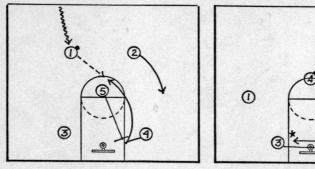

Diagram 5-6

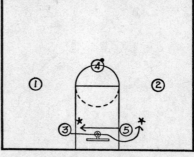

Diagram 5-7

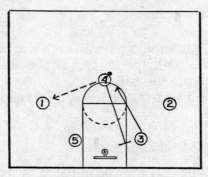

Diagram 5-8

PASS-TO-POST CONTINUITY PLAY

This play begins when (1) passes to post man, (5), and splits the post with the other guard, (2). To clear the lane, both forwards come out front. See Diagram 5-9.

After this movement, the post man gives the ball off to one of the forwards, (in this case, (4) in Diagram 5-10). This pass signals the guards to cross inside.

(4) looks inside for (2) coming across the lane. If (2) isn't open, (4) passes the ball to (5), who has cut toward the basket and back to the ball as in Diagram 5-11.

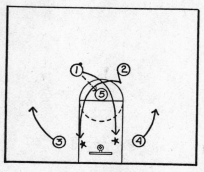

Diagram 5-9

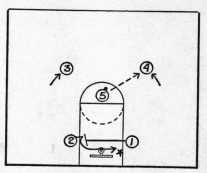

Diagram 5-10

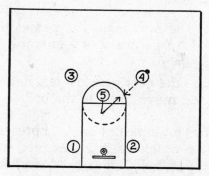

Diagram 5-11

In Diagram 5-12, the sequence continues as both forwards, (3) and (4), pinch inside with down screens for (1) and (2).

As soon as (5) passes to either guard, the forwards cross inside. See Diagram 5-13.

So, in effect, the rules for this play are:

a. When the guards, (1) and (2), pass the ball to the post, they split and cut to the basket while the forwards, (3) and (4), clear high.

b. When the forwards, (3) and (4), pass to the post, they pinch inside for the guards.

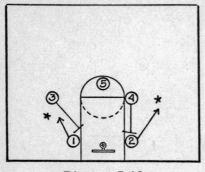

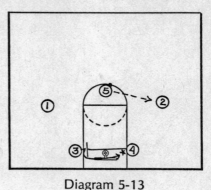

Diagram 5-12   Diagram 5-13

c. Anytime the post man, (5), passes to a high man, whether he be a guard or a forward, the two inside men exchange.

d. Everytime the post man passes, he cuts toward the basket and moves back to the ball.

This play has multiple options and presents the defense with many varied problems. It is designed for a disciplined team that can stay in their patterns and work for a good shot.

THE DOUBLE DOWN TO FLEX CONTINUITY PLAY

(1) passes to the post and both he and (2) screen down for their respective forwards. (3) and (4) break out and in Diagram 5-14, (5) passes to (3).

This tells (1), the inside man on (3)'s side, to back out to the corner and it informs the far inside man, (2), to set a screen on (4)'s defender. See Diagram 5-15.

(3) may shoot or pass to (4), cutting to the basket. (5) then screens down for (2). See Diagram 5-16.

These movements put the team in the flex continuity offense. (3) can pass to (2) and the play continues as Diagram 5-17 shows.

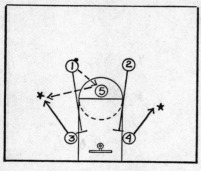

Diagram 5-14

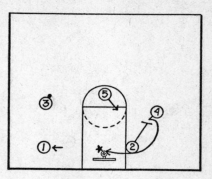

Diagram 5-15

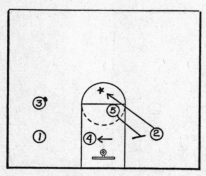

Diagram 5-16

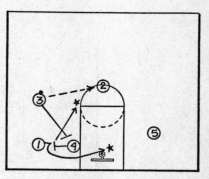

Diagram 5-17

DOUBLE SCREEN PLAY

This play is keyed when guard, (1), passes to high-post man, (5). The ballside forward, (3), goes backdoor and both guards screen away for the offside forward, (4). See Diagram 5-18.

If (5) passes to (3), he usually has a lay-up shot. When (5) passes to (4) coming out, he screens down for (3). At the same time, (1) ducks around (2) and the result is, in effect, a double stack. See Diagram 5-19.

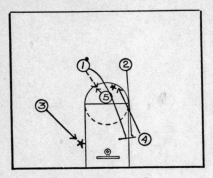

Diagram 5-18

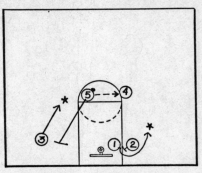

Diagram 5-19

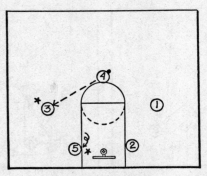

Diagram 5-20

If (4) passes to (3) or (1), they may shoot or look for the teammate in their respective post area. See Diagram 5-20.

THE UP-AND-DOWN PLAY

This play starts when (1) passes to (5) and cuts directly to screen for (4), the offside forward. (4) uses the screen and cuts up to the free throw line. At the same time, the offside guard, (2), starts the crossing motion. But this time, the onside for-

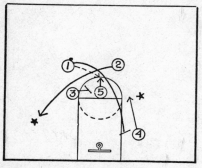

Diagram 5-21

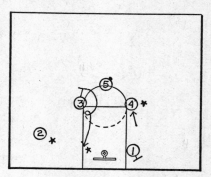

Diagram 5-22

ward, (3), has moved up to screen (2)'s defender as he cuts by wide and toward the corner. See Diagram 5-21.

(3) then rolls, and (5) may pass to (4) coming off (1)'s screen to (2) for a jump shot in the corner, or to (3) rolling to the basket. See Diagram 5-22.

THE SPLIT LOB PLAY

In this play, (1) passes to (5) and starts his splitting movement with (2). Seeing this, the offside forward, (4), quickly moves to the free throw line. The onside forward, (3), who was probably being overplayed, backdoors to the onside low-post area and stops. (2) starts his crossing motion. See Diagram 5-23.

(5) looks first for (3) on the backdoor cut. By then, (1) has cut off (4) and may be open for a lob pass as in Diagram 5-24.

If neither (3) nor (1) are open, (2) continues his cut and screens for (3), who moves out for a possible jump shot. (2) rolls inside. On the offside, after (1) has cut and cleared, (4) rolls inside. (5) must hit the open man as Diagram 5-25 illustrates.

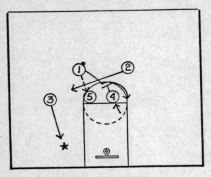

Diagram 5-23

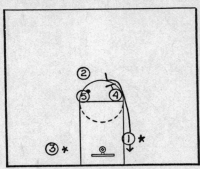

Diagram 5-24

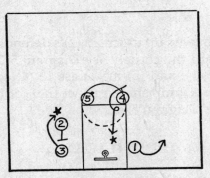

Diagram 5-25

THE WIDE SPLIT PLAY

This play begins as guard, (1), passes to the high-post man, (5), at the head of the key and splits the post with the offside guard, (2). Forwards (3) and (4) pinch in and screen for the guards who move toward the corners. After screening, forwards (3) and (4) roll to their respective lay-up slots. See Diagram 5-26.

(5) may pass either to a forward inside or to a guard who may have lost his man on the screen. When the ball is passed to a guard (as to (2) in Diagram 5-27), the high-post man, (5),

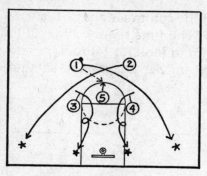

Diagram 5-26

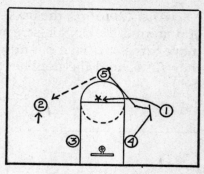

Diagram 5-27

and the offside forward, (4), screen for the offside guard who breaks to the head of the key.

THE HIGH SCREEN PLAY

This time the offside forward, (4), moves up to screen for the offside guard, (2), as the pass is made from (1) to (5). After passing, (1) moves down to form the double screen along with (3). (5) looks first for (2) cutting to the basket off (4)'s screen. See Diagram 5-28.

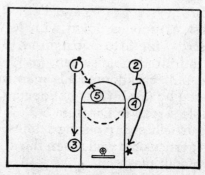

Diagram 5-28

After (2) cuts to the basket, he continues across the lane and around the double screen. The time required for (2) to move across the lane permits (5) to look for (4) rolling, and then (2) behind the double screen. See Diagrams 5-29 and 5-30.

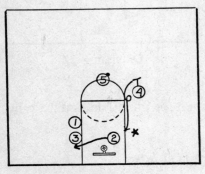

Diagram 5-29

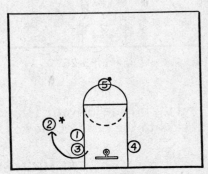

Diagram 5-30

BACKDOOR FAKE SPLIT PLAY

After the guards have passed to the high post and split several times, a special backdoor option may be run with great success. (1) again passes to (5), and both (1) and (2) fake splitting the post. (1) moves down with forward, (4), and forms a double screen for (3) to loop around. (3) clears his side and comes around the double screen. (5) looks first for (2), who faked the split, backdoored his man, and cut to the lay-up slot vacated by (3). If (2) is not open, (5) looks for (3) behind the double screen in Diagram 5-31.

This play is usually set up during a time-out or by a hand signal. It works particularly well when the defensive guards are switching on split plays.

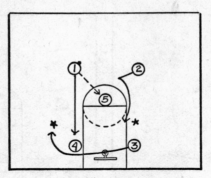

Diagram 5-31

THE TRIPLE SCREEN PLAY

This play is run when the onside forward, (3), is getting a great deal of overplay. (3) calls, "clear" and cuts low toward the lane. This tells the post man, (5), to step out wide and receive a pass from (1). See Diagram 5-32.

Then (1), (2), and (3) move to triple-screen (4)'s defender with (2) in the middle. See Diagram 5-33.

(4) may now cut high or low. Whichever way (4) goes, (1)

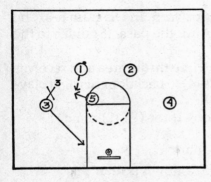

Diagram 5-32

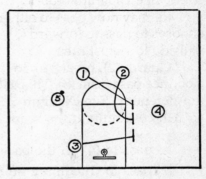

Diagram 5-33

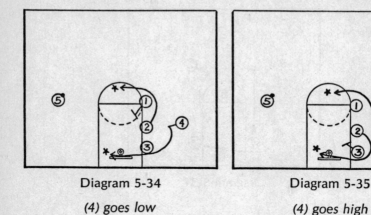

Diagram 5-34   Diagram 5-35

(4) goes low   *(4) goes high*

and (4) will pinch in on (2)'s defender, and (2) will go opposite. See Diagrams 5-34 and 5-35 for illustrations of these
maneuvers.

THE DOUBLE-DOWN BACKDOOR PLAY

This play begins when guard, (1), passes to post man, (5).
Both guards, (1) and (2), then screen down for their respective
forward. The forwards, (3) and (4), move out toward midcourt. See Diagram 5-36.

(5) may now pass to either forward. In Diagram 5-37, he
chooses to pass to forward (3). After the pass, (5) slides to the
ballside low-post area.

Guard, (2), breaks up to the free throw area and receives
a bounce pass from (3). This tells (4) to backdoor his overplaying defender. See Diagram 5-38.

In continuity, (3) screens down for (1). (2) may:

a. pass to (4) on the backdoor cut
b. pass to (1) coming off (3)'s down screen
c. look for (5) in the low-post area.

See Diagram 5-39.

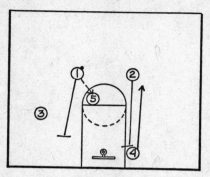

Diagram 5-36

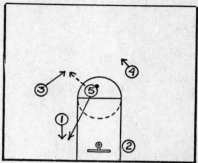

Diagram 5-37

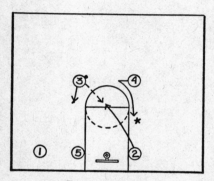

Diagram 5-38

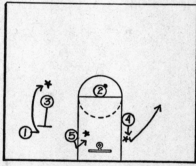

Diagram 5-39

6

PLAYS KEYED BY A DIAGONAL CUT

A diagonal cut is when a guard passes to the forward on his side and cuts diagonally down the free throw lane. It is very functional for teams with a strong post man because the direction of the cut temporarily hinders the offside help and provides a time to work post-oriented plays. Following are some diagonal cut plays.

THE DIAGONAL CUT CONTINUITY PLAY

This continuity begins as guard, (1), passes to forward, (3), and makes a diagonal cut down the lane. This tells post man, (5), to swing to the ballside medium-post area. Forward, (4), uses (1)'s cut as a natural screen and cuts to the ballside high-post area. In the event (4) is open, (3) may pass to him for a jump shot at the free throw line. After his cut, (1) moves to the offside wing area. (2) also moves away from the ball. See Diagram 6-1.

(3) may now:

a. Pass to (5) and screen for (4). After screening, (3) rolls down the middle as shown in Diagram 6-2.
b. Keep the continuity going by passing to (2) as he moves toward the ball as shown in Diagram 6-3.

In turn, (2) reverses the ball to (1) at the wing; (3) cuts to the ball; (5) swings to the ballside low-post area; and (4) takes (3)'s former side. See Diagram 6-4.

In Diagram 6-5, the play continues as (2) screens diagonally for (4), who moves toward the ball.

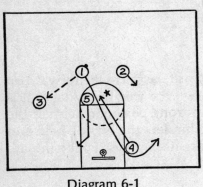

Diagram 6-1

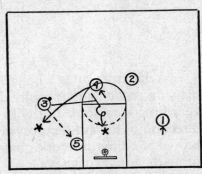

Diagram 6-2

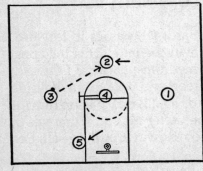

Diagram 6-3

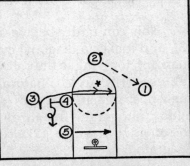

Diagram 6-4

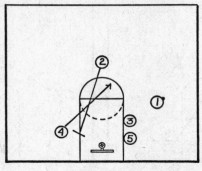

Diagram 6-5

(1)'s options are:

a. Pass to (3) for a jump shot at the free throw line.
b. Pass to (5) and split the post with (3).
c. Keep the continuity going by passing to (4), who would then reverse the ball to (2).

Forward-Posting Option

When a forward is superior to his defender in the post area, the forward-posting option may be run. In Diagram 6-6 the forward, (4), can dominate his defensive man. Knowing this the post man, (5), on the initial pass from (1) to (3), clears the ballside medium-post area and swings to the offside post area. This allows (4) to use (1)'s natural screen and swing to the ballside low-post area and take advantage of the mismatch. See Diagram 6-6.

In the event (4) does get a shot, (5) (who is probably a big man) is in good position to rebound.

If (4) is not open, (2) moves to the ball, (3) passes to him and hesitates until (4) screens for (3); as soon as (2) passed to (1), the continuity would go on. Note how (3) dipped after passing to (2). This move facilitates (4)'s screen. See Diagrams 6-7 and 6-8.

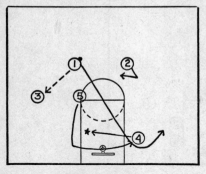

Diagram 6-6

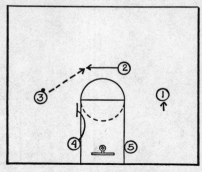

Diagram 6-7

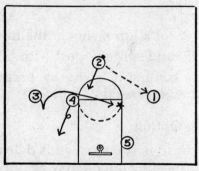

Diagram 6-8

THE PORTLAND DIAGONAL CUT SERIES

This play begins with (1) passing to (3) and cutting diagonally to screen for the offside forward, (4). (4) cuts to the head of the key, and (1) rolls to the ballside low-post area. (2) dips toward the basket and then clears to the offside wing area. See Diagram 6-9.

(3) may now:

a. Pass to (5) and split the post with his choice of either (1) or (4), while the other backdoors his defender and

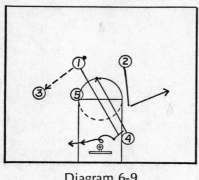

Diagram 6-9

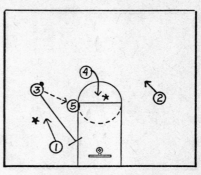

Diagram 6-10

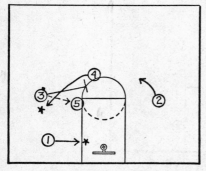

Diagram 6-11

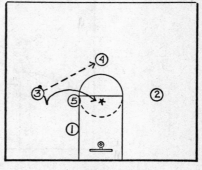

Diagram 6-12

cuts to the basket as Diagrams 6-10 and 6-11 show. In Diagram 6-10, (3) splits with (1) and (4) backdoors. In Diagram 6-11, (3) splits with (4) and (1) backdoors.

b. Pass to (4). When this happens, (3) cuts off (5) and looks for a quick return pass from (4) as Diagram 6-12 shows.

If (3) is not open, (4) may pass to (1), moving out of a down screen from (5). (4) may also pass to (2) in this series. See Diagram 6-13.

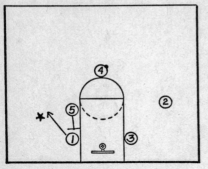

Diagram 6-13

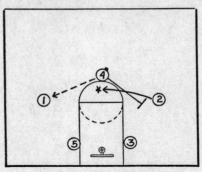

Diagram 6-14

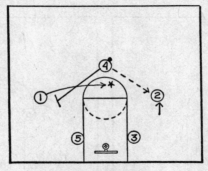

Diagram 6-15

If (4) passes to (1), he screens opposite for (2). See Diagram 6-14.

If (4) passes to (2), he screens opposite for (1). See Diagram 6-15.

The High-Low Change-Up Options

When running the Portland Diagonal Cut Play, a very functional option that may be added is the high-low change-up.

This option occurs after (1) has passed to (3), screened down diagonally for (4) (who moved to the head of the key), and rolled to the ballside low-post area. (Refer to Diagram 6-9.)

(3) now has the ball (Diagram 6-16) and will pass the ball to (4) and then cut. When using this option, (3) may do one of two things:

a. He may pass to (4) and cut over (5) and (1). This is followed by the standard option as shown in Diagram 6-16 and Diagram 6-17.

b. (3) may pass to (4) and screen down for (1) in the ballside low-post area. (1) then starts to pop out to the wing position, but instead he cuts over (5), looking for a pass from (4). If he does not receive it, he continues to the far low-post area. See Diagram 6-18.

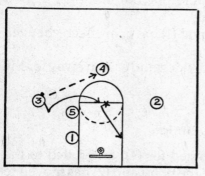

Diagram 6-16

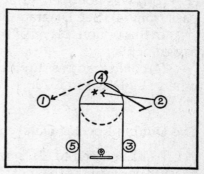

Diagram 6-17

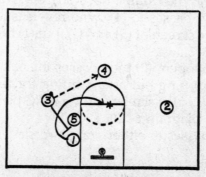

Diagram 6-18

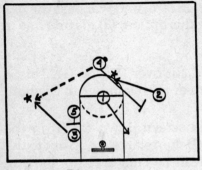

Diagram 6-19

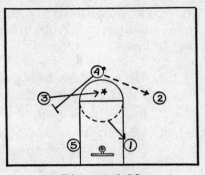

Diagram 6-20

If (1) was not open, (3) would pop out to the wing for a pass from (4). See Diagram 6-19.

In this option, players (3) and (1) have, in effect, changed assignments.

(4) could then pass to either wing and screen away for the other. See Diagram 6-20.

The Double Reverse Delayed Option

(1) has passed to (3), screened for (4), and rolled to the ballside post area. (4) has cut to the point and (2) has moved to the offside wing area. (Refer to Diagram 6-9.)

From there, the Double Reverse Delayed Option may be run. (3) quickly passes to (4), who reverses it to (2). (3) cuts over the double screen of (5) and (1), but (1) does not pop out. See Diagram 6-21.

If (3) is not open, (2) then passes the ball back to (4) who looks for (1) popping out after waiting for the ball to be returned to (4). (2) also screens down for (3) who pops out on that side. See Diagram 6-22.

(4) then passes to either wing and screens away for the other.

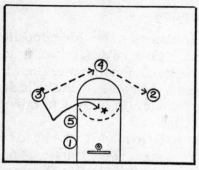

Diagram 6-21

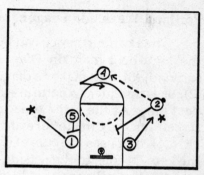

Diagram 6-22

The Quick-Up Lob Option

This play begins with (1) passing to (3) and making his diagonal cut down the lane. But this time, the offside forward, (4), has made the quick-up move and sets a screen on (1)'s defender. (1) utilizes this screen by cutting to the basket for a lob pass from (3). See Diagram 6-23.

If (1) is not open for the lob, he moves to the ballside low-post area. (4) moves to the head of the key, and the basic Portland options are again available. See Diagram 6-24.

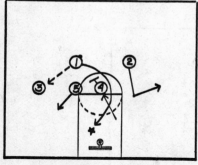

Diagram 6-23

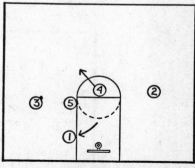

Diagram 6-24

Portland Weakside Diagonal Option

The Portland series can be initiated on the side opposite the high-post man. In Diagram 6-25, guard, (1), passes to forward, (3), and makes a diagonal cut down the lane. Guard, (2), uses this cut as a natural screen as he moves to the ballside post area. At the same time, post man, (5), moves to down screen for the offside forward, (4).

(4) then uses the cuts of (5) and (1) to move to the head of the key. (1) rolls to the offside wing area. See Diagram 6-26.

(5) then rolls to the ballside high-post area. See Diagram 6-27.

From there, the two basic Portland options may be run.

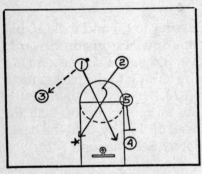

Diagram 6-25

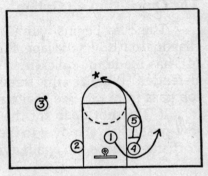

Diagram 6-26

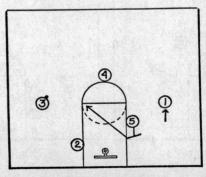

Diagram 6-27

THE WEAKSIDE DIAGONAL PLAY

This is a one-time around, quick-hitter type of play. It is initiated on the side of the floor opposite the high-post man. The play is keyed when guard, (1), passes to forward, (3), and cuts diagonally down the lane. This tells the offside forward, (4), who sets up high on this play, to cut off post man, (5), and to the ballside low-post area. See Diagram 6-28.

If (4) is not open, (3) passes to (2) who moves toward the ball; (5) screens down for (1) who hesitated in the low-post area. See Diagram 6-29.

(2) may also pass to (1) moving out of (5)'s down screen. (1) may shoot or pass to (5) in the low-post area. In the event (2) cannot get the ball to (1), (3) also screens down for (4). See Diagram 6-30.

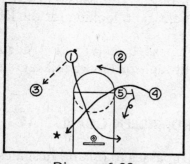

Diagram 6-28

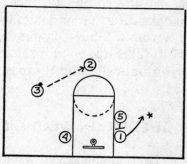

Diagram 6-29

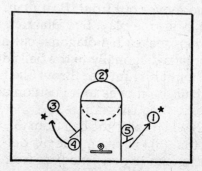

Diagram 6-30

DIAGONAL CUT LOB SEQUENCE

Play #1

(1) passes to (3) and fakes an outside cut. This brings the offside forward, (4), across the lane. (2) then changes direction and attempts to rub his defender off on the high-post man, (5). This may get him open for a lob pass from (3). (2) clears to the ballside corner. See Diagram 6-31.

If (1) is not open for the lob pass, both (5) and (4) move across the lane to screen for him. He may go over or under the double screen as seen in Diagram 6-32.

Play #2

(1) passes to (3), makes the outside fake, and then cuts to the ballside corner. (2) fakes cutting to the ballside corner, changes direction and cuts to the basket, looking for the lob pass from (3). See Diagram 6-33.

If (2) is not open for the lob pass, both (5) and (4) again screen opposite and (2) may cut high or low. See Diagram 6-34.

THE DIAGONAL CUT-GUARD, SCREEN-GUARD PLAY

This play is keyed when (1) passes to (3) and hesitates. This tells (2), the offside guard, to screen down for the offside forward, (4), who moves out front. Post man, (5), drops low for a possible one-on-one play. See Diagram 6-35.

Guard (1) then makes his diagonal cut and screens for guard (2) who breaks diagonally to the ballside of the key. If (2) is open, (3) should hit him free throw line high. If (2) does not receive the ball, he moves to a position above the circle and on the ballside. See Diagram 6-36.

At times, (2) will receive the ball from (3), turn to face the basket and find that (5) is open inside his defender who may have been fronting him to deny the pass from (3). When this

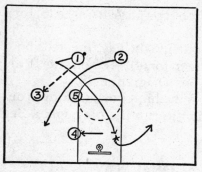

Diagram 6-31

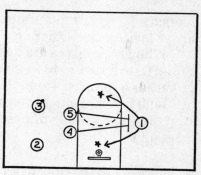

Diagram 6-32

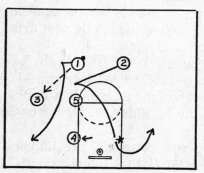

Diagram 6-33

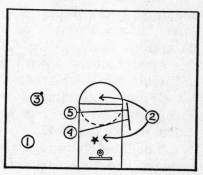

Diagram 6-34

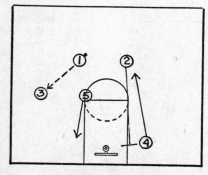

Diagram 6-35

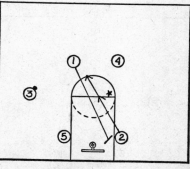

Diagram 6-36

happens, (2) will drop a jump shot-type pass inside to (5) for a power lay-up. See Diagram 6-37.

When (2) receives the ball outside the key, this tells both (5) and (1) to move up high to screen for (4). (4) then cuts to the basket for a lob pass from (2). See Diagram 6-38.

If (4) is not open, (5) stays in the high post, (1) moves out front, and the team is in position to run the play again. See Diagram 6-39.

THE DOUBLE DIAGONAL PLAY

This play begins with post man, (5), in the center of the free throw circle. (1) passes to (3) and starts his diagonal cut down the lane. This time he is joined in the cut by post man, (5), and the offside guard, (2). See Diagram 6-40.

About halfway down the lane, (2) cuts back to the ball and attempts to lose his man on (1) and (5). See Diagram 6-41.

(1) and (5) continue down the lane and form a double screen for (4) who swings to the ballside low-post area as shown in Diagram 6-42.

If neither (2) nor (4) are open, (2) changes direction and comes back to receive a pass from (3). (1) then loops around (5) and (3) screens down for (4). (2) passes to the open man. See Diagram 6-43.

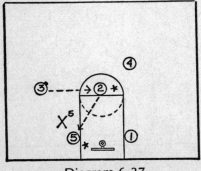

Diagram 6-37

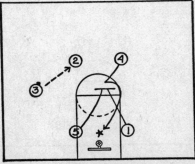

Diagram 6-38

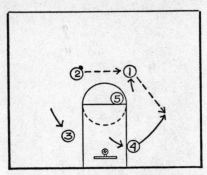

Diagram 6-39

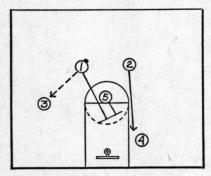

Diagram 6-40

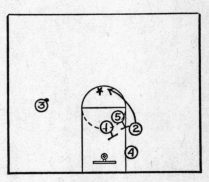

Diagram 6-41

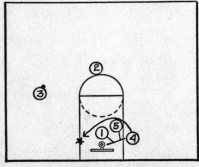

Diagram 6-42

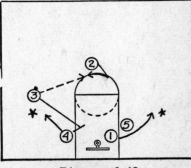

Diagram 6-43

.7 | DOUBLE-CUT PLAYS

The idea of sending both guards through at one time has much merit. Among its attributes are: it removes the saggers and helpers from the front of the defense, it makes it difficult for the opponents to fast break by putting their potential outlet men in adverse positions, and it doubles the number of initial cutters who must be accounted for. The following double-cut plays have a lot of functional movement and some of them may be used against zone defenses.

THE DOUBLE INSIDE-CUT PLAY

This is the basic double-cut play. It begins when guard, (1), passes to his forward, (3), and makes a sweeping cut to the offside low-post area. He may possibly be open on a give-and-go type move. As soon as (1) has cleared the ballside low-post area, the offside guard, (2), makes a slash cut off the high-post man, (5), to the ballside low-post area. See Diagram 7-1.

If neither is open, (5) screens opposite for the offside forward, (4), who moves to the head of the key for a possible shot. See Diagram 7-2.

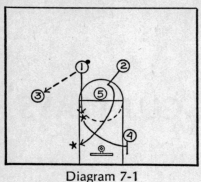

Diagram 7-1

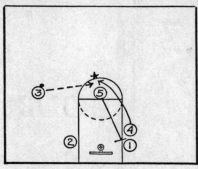

Diagram 7-2

As soon as (3) passes to (4), (1) pops out on the far side, and (3) screens down for (2). See Diagram 7-3.

(4) may pass to (2) or (1) and at times can even whip the ball inside to (3) or (5). In Diagram 7-4, (1) received the ball from (4). He could at this point shoot, look for (5) posting inside, or look for (2) coming to the point off of a screen by (4). (4) is instructed to always screen opposite after passing to a wing.

At that point the man in the ballside post area, (5), screens opposite for the man in the offside post area, (3). See Diagram 7-5.

If nothing develops, (1) dribbles out front, (5) moves to the high-post position and the team is in position to run a new play. See Diagram 7-6.

THE STRAIGHT-THROUGH DOUBLE-CUT PLAY

Guard, (1), passes to forward, (3), and he and the offside guard, (2), cut through simultaneously. (2) cuts straight to the blocks on his side and (1) swings to (2)'s side. See Diagram 7-7.

(4), the offside forward, uses guards (2) and (1) as he cuts over them and to the ballside low-post area as shown in Diagram 7-8.

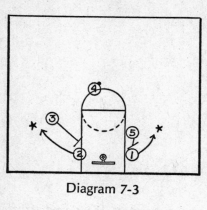

Diagram 7-3

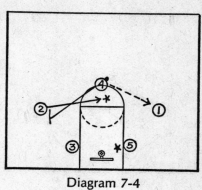

Diagram 7-4

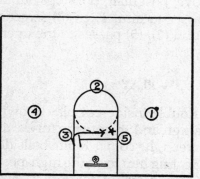

Diagram 7-5

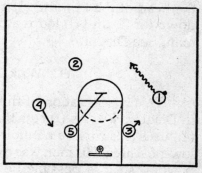

Diagram 7-6

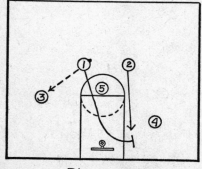

Diagram 7-7

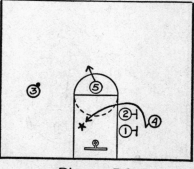

Diagram 7-8

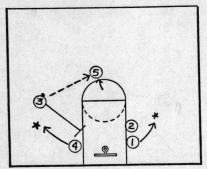

Diagram 7-9

If (4) is not open in this move, post man, (5), steps out to the head of the key and (3) passes to him. Then (3) screens down for (4) and (1) loops around (2). (5) passes to the open man. See Diagram 7-9.

FORWARD LOW PLAY

This is a variation of the double inside-cut play shown in Diagram 7-1. As (1) cuts through and the offside forward, (4), uses (1)'s cut as a natural screen, he comes to the ballside low-post area. His man was expecting him to go the high-post position so it is possible he may be completely open. See Diagram 7-10.

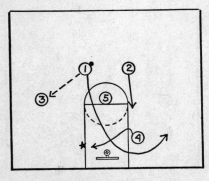

Diagram 7-10

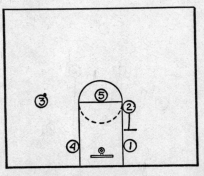

Diagram 7-11

(2), who expected to cut to the ballside post area, moves to replace (4) in his original offside forward position. See Diagram 7-11.

If (4) is not open, (5) screens opposite for (2) and the same options (with players exchanging assignments) are run. See Diagrams 7-12 through 7-17 for these options.

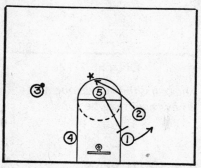

Diagram 7-12

(5) screens away for (2), who moves to the head of the key.

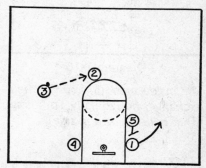

Diagram 7-13

(3) passes to (2); (5) jams down and (1) pops out.

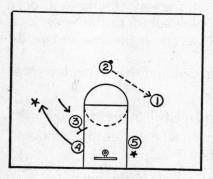

Diagram 7-14

The ball is then passed to (1), moving to the wing, as (3) jams down and (4) pops out on the other (weak) side.

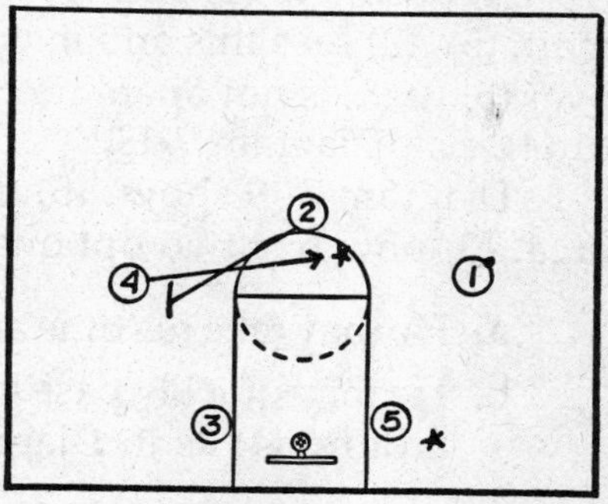

Diagram 7-15

After his pass to (1), (2) screens away for (4).

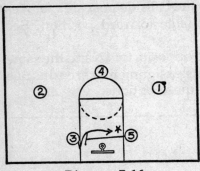

Diagram 7-16

The inside men, (5) and (3), then exchange horizontally, bringing (3) to ballside (strong side).

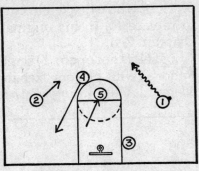

Diagram 7-17

The ball is then taken out front and a new play may be run.

GUARD-LOOP DOUBLE-CUT PLAY

This play works well when used with the basic double-cut play.

(1) passes to (3) and loops all the way around high-post man, (5). (2) sees this and makes his cut for the low-post area over (5). If (2) is not open, he clears across the lane and inside of (4). See Diagram 7-18.

Diagram 7-19 shows (5) dropping down to the low-post area. (3) now has two options:

a. He may take his time and feed (5) in the low-post area.
b. He may quickly pass to (1), who passes to (2), looping around (4) as in Diagram 7-20.

(2) may then shoot or look for (4) in the post.

DOUBLE-CUT SPLIT PLAY

This play begins as (1) passes to his forward, (3), and makes a diagonal cut. The offside guard, (2), is a scoring

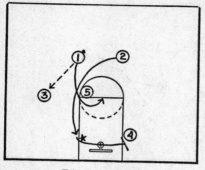

Diagram 7-18   Diagram 7-19

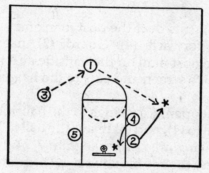

Diagram 7-20

option as he slashes over post man, (5), to the ballside low-post area and then clears across the lane. Forward, (4), uses (1)'s cut as a natural screen and moves to the head of the key. (1) also clears to the offside wing. See Diagram 7-21.

If (4) or (2) are not open, (3) passes to (5) in the post and splits the post with (4) as Diagram 7-22 illustrates.

(1) goes to the point to maintain defensive balance.

DOUBLE-CUT TO SHUFFLE PLAY

One of the best plays keyed by a double cut is Garland Pinholster's pinwheel shuffle. It starts as guard, (1), passes to

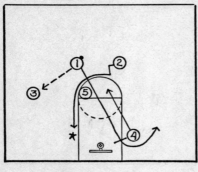

Diagram 7-21

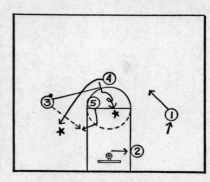

Diagram 7-22

his forward, (3), cuts over the post man and moves to screen for the offside forward, (4). Guard, (2), uses (1)'s cut and moves over the post man on the ballside and to the low-post area. (4) uses (1)'s screen and cuts to the head of the key. See Diagram 7-23.

If (2) is not open, (5) swings to the ballside three-quarter post, (3) passes to (4), and (4) relays the ball to (1), moving out to the offside wing area. See Diagram 7-24.

From there, the shuffle shown in Diagrams 7-25 through 7-27 is run.

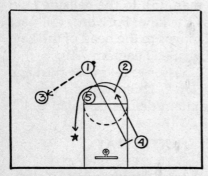

Diagram 7-23

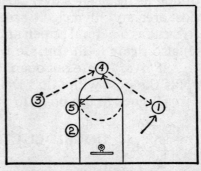

Diagram 7-24

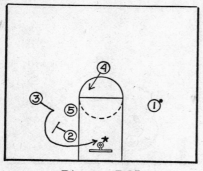

Diagram 7-25

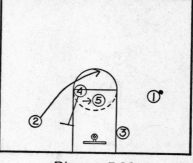

Diagram 7-26

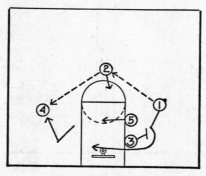

Diagram 7-27

Forward-Across Option

A variation that may be added to this shuffle play is the Forward-Across Option. It is activated when (1) passes to (3) and screens for (4). This time, however, (4) swings to the ballside low-post area. (2) starts his cut, but doubles back to the head of the key. See Diagram 7-28.

(5) then swings to the ballside three-quarter post area. (3) looks first for (4), and if he isn't open, passes to (2) out front to start the shuffle. See Diagrams 7-29 through 7-31.

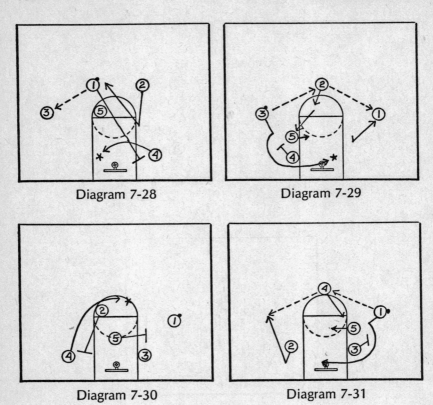

Diagram 7-28   Diagram 7-29

Diagram 7-30   Diagram 7-31

FIRST GUARD INSIDE FORWARD-ACROSS PLAY

Guard, (1), passes to forward, (3), makes an inside cut and then moves to the ballside corner. (2), the offside guard, cuts over the post man across the lane and screens for the offside forward, (4), who swings across the lane. See Diagrams 7-32 and 7-33.

If (4) is not open, (5) screens away for (2), who comes to the point. (3) passes to (2) and screens down for (1). See Diagram 7-34.

(3) then cuts to the far side, (5) moves to the high post and the team is in position to run a new play. See Diagram 7-35.

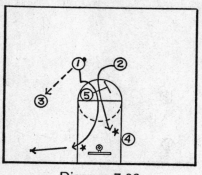

Diagram 7-32

Diagram 7-33

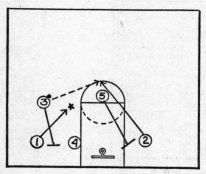

Diagram 7-34

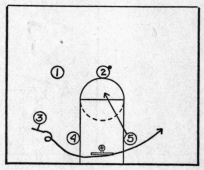

Diagram 7-35

THE DOUBLE-CUT CLEAR PLAY

This time (1) passes to (3), cuts over (5) and clears to the ballside corner. (2) sees this and cuts over (5) to the ballside post area. See Diagrams 7-36 and 7-37.

If (2) is not open, he continues across the lane and around (4). At the same time, (5) steps out and works a screen-and-roll play with (3). See Diagram 7-38.

(3) may shoot, pass to (5) on the roll, or pass to (2) looping around (4).

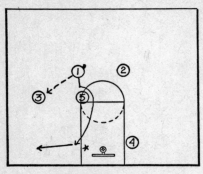

Diagram 7-36

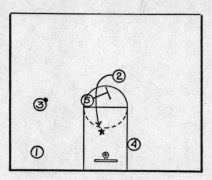

Diagram 7-37

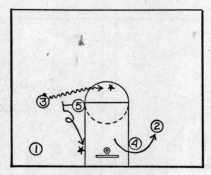

Diagram 7-38

DOUBLE-CUT TO REVERSE-ACTION PLAY

This play begins with guard, (1), passing to forward, (3), slashing off the post to the ballside lay-up area and then clearing to the corner. Guard, (2), moves toward the ballside, and post man, (5), prepares to screen for him. See Diagram 7-39.

In Diagram 7-40 (2) then slashes over (5) on the ballside

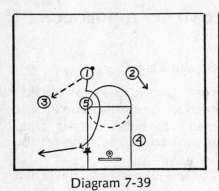

Diagram 7-39

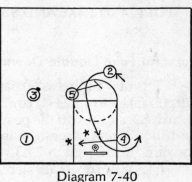

Diagram 7-40

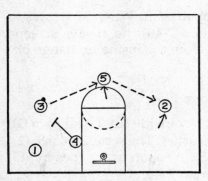

Diagram 7-41

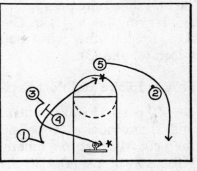

Diagram 7-42

and clears across the lane to form a natural screen for (4). (4) uses this screen and cuts to the ballside.

If (2) or (4) are not open, (5) steps out to the head of the key, and (3) passes to him. (5) then passes to (2), and (4) steps out to screen for (3). See Diagram 7-41.

After passing to (2), (5) makes an outside cut to the ballside corner. (3) cuts off (4) and (1) uses both of them to cut to the point. See Diagram 7-42. From there, the reverse action continuity may be run.

FORWARD FAKE AND SECOND GUARD THROUGH SERIES

Forward Fake Double Down Screen Play

This play begins as (1) passes to (3) and makes an outside cut. (3) fakes to (1) as (1) continues to the corner. The offside guard, (2), slashes off the post man to the ballside lay-up area, and then clears across the lane and around (4), the offside forward. See Diagram 7-43.

If (2) is not open, (5) steps out and (3) passes to him. Then (3) screens down for (1), and (2) loops around (4). See Diagram 7-44.

(5) then may pass to the open man. When he passes to either wing (as to (2) in Diagram 7-45), he always screens away for the other wing man. Note the inside exchange between (4) and (3).

Forward Fake and Post Exchange Play

(1) passes to (3) and makes an outside cut. (3) fakes to (1), and (1) continues to the ballside corner. The second guard, (2), then cuts off high-post man, (5). As soon as (2) goes by, (5) screens away for (4). See Diagram 7-46.

If (2) is not open on his slash cut, he continues across the lane and around (5). (4) uses (5)'s screen to move to the head of the key. See Diagram 7-47.

In Diagram 7-48, (5) rolls to the ballside.

(3) may now:

a. Pass to (4) and screen down for (1). (4) could then pass to (1) coming off (3)'s screen or reverse the ball to (2) as in Diagram 7-49.

b. Pass to (5) and screen for (1) or (4). Whichever one (3) chose to screen for, the other would backdoor. Diagram 7-50 shows (3) screening for (4) and (1) making the backdoor cut.

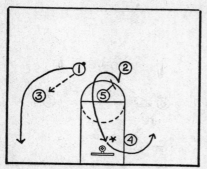

Diagram 7-43

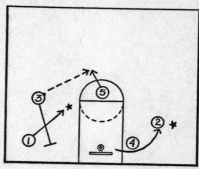

Diagram 7-44

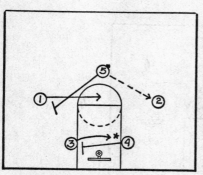

Diagram 7-45

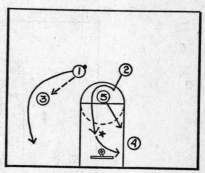

Diagram 7-46

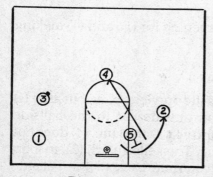

Diagram 7-47

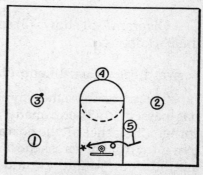

Diagram 7-48

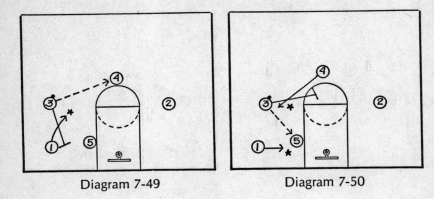

Diagram 7-49   Diagram 7-50

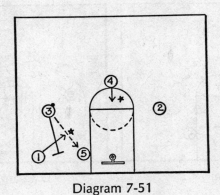

Diagram 7-51

Diagram 7-51 shows (3) screening for (1), and (4) making the backdoor cut.

Forward Fake Guard Loop Play

This starts the same way as the previous play, but after (1) has passed to (3) and made an outside cut to the ballside corner, (2) slashes off the post and across the lane. (4) does not move out front or across the lane. This tells guard, (2), to loop around both (4) and (5) and continue back to the ballside low-post area. See Diagram 7-52.

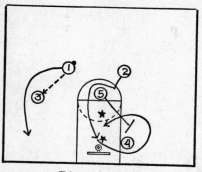

Diagram 7-52

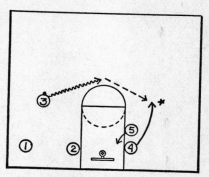

Diagram 7-53

If (2) is not open, (3) dribbles to the head of the key and looks for (4) popping out of (5)'s down screen. See Diagram 7-53.

A note of caution should be added at this point. Sending both guards through can make a team vulnerable to fast breaks. Much practice time must be spent on maintaining defensive balance.

8

MAN-TO-MAN PRESSURE RELIEVERS

The day of bringing the ball up-court and having no trouble initiating your man-to-man offense is over. Opponents will overplay the ballside and you can count on it. To counteract this, team techniques must be created that put the pressuring team at a disadvantage. Following are some play-initiating pressure moves that may be utilized versus man-to-man defenses.

BACKDOOR LOB

Seeing that the ballside guard, (1), is unable to get the ball to forward, (3), or post man, (5), the offside forward, (4), breaks up to the free throw line and receives a bounce pass. After the pass, (1) slashes to the outside off (5) for a possible lob pass. At the same time, the offside guard, (2), attempts to backdoor his defender. See Diagram 8-1.

If neither (1) nor (2) is open, (5) screens away for (3), who has dipped toward the baseline, and (1) cuts across the lane and around (2) who screens down for him. (4) passes to the open man. See Diagram 8-2.

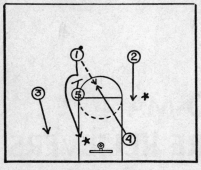 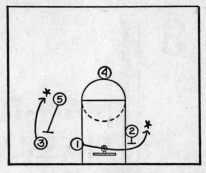

Diagram 8-1   Diagram 8-2

THE FORWARD ACROSS

When it becomes apparent that the ball cannot be passed from guard to forward to start the offense, the ballside forward, (3), clears down and around the offside forward, (4). The guard with the ball, (1), then reverses it by way of guard (2) to (3) as he loops around (4). See Diagram 8-3.

This tells forward, (4), to screen opposite for post man, (5), as in Diagram 8-4.

The team is now in position to run an offensive play. At times, X3 will hustle and beat (3) around (4)'s screen. When this happens, (3) can sometimes double back and take a pass from one of the guards for an easy shot. See Diagram 8-5.

FORWARD OVER

Again, guard, (1), cannot get the ball to his forward, (3). Seeing this, post man, (5), steps out and screens for (3), who cuts over him. (1) may be able to pass to (3) coming over the top. In this case, (3) can shoot or look for (5) on the roll. See Diagram 8-6.

If (1) cannot pass to (3), it is usually because (5)'s defender

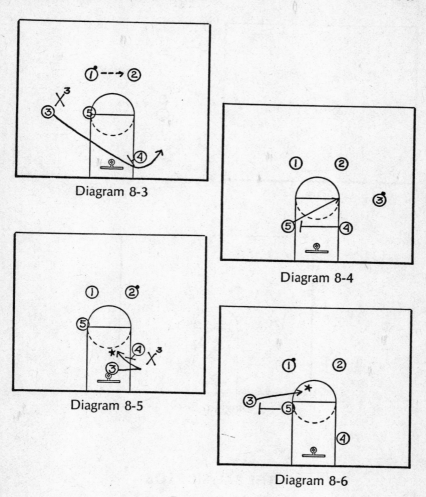

Diagram 8-3

Diagram 8-4

Diagram 8-5

Diagram 8-6

has helped by hedging on (3). This leaves (5) wide open, so (1) passes to (5) to initiate the play. See Diagrams 8-7 and 8-8.

(3) then continues across and screens for (4), who swings to the ballside post position. See Diagram 8-9.

In effect, (5) and (4) have changed positions. The team is in position to run a play.

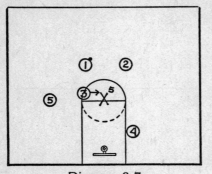

Diagram 8-7

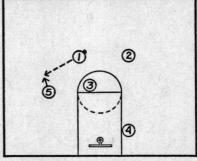

Diagram 8-8

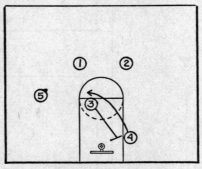

Diagram 8-9

THE BALLSIDE LOB

Since guard, (1), cannot get the ball to his forward, (3), the offside forward breaks to the high-post area and calls, "Ball." See Diagram 8-10.

This takes away the primary offside defensive helper, (4), and gives (3) the opportunity to backdoor X3 and receive a lob pass from (1). See Diagram 8-11.

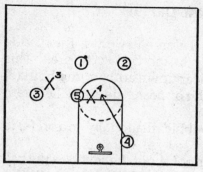

Diagram 8-10

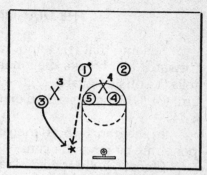

Diagram 8-11

THE ROTATION MOVE

The rotation move begins when guard, (1), is stopped either in the back court or very high in the front court. His forward (3), breaks almost to midcourt and receives a pass from (1). See Diagram 8-12.

At this time, (4), the offside forward, comes across and replaces (3), and the offside guard, (2), rotates to the offside forward position. See Diagram 8-13.

In effect, (3) and (2) have exchanged guard and forward positions and now the offense may be run.

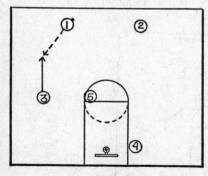

Diagram 8-12

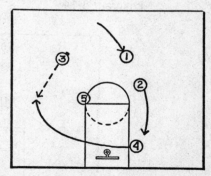

Diagram 8-13

THE DIAGONAL DRIBBLE

Sensing that (1) cannot make an entry pass, the offside forward, (4), breaks diagonally to the high-post area. This tells the offside guard, (2), to clear down and around both (5) and (3), who have stacked on the opposite side. See Diagram 8-14.

In Diagram 8-15, (1) then dribbles diagonally and off (4) to penetrate as far as he can.

Once (1) is stopped and cannot shoot, he reverses the ball to (2), behind (3) and (5)'s double screen, by way of (4). See Diagram 8-16.

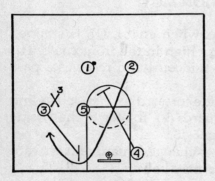

Diagram 8-14

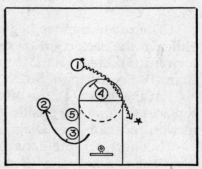

Diagram 8-15

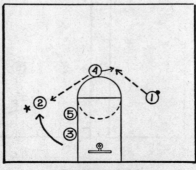

Diagram 8-16

THE GUARD LOOP

Seeing that (1) cannot get the ball to (3), the guard, (2), keys the play by looping around the high-post man, (5). See Diagram 8-17 for this maneuver.

As shown in Diagram 8-17, this move also keys the offside forward, (4), to clear across the lane.

Guard, (1), then dribbles off (5), who has stepped out and set a definite screen. (1) penetrates as far as he can, then looks for (3) cutting toward him off (4)'s screen. See Diagrams 8-18 and 8-19.

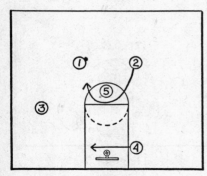

Diagram 8-17

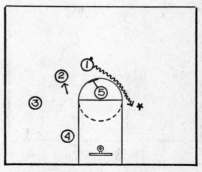

Diagram 8-18

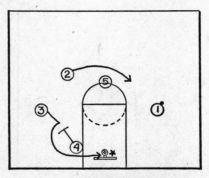

Diagram 8-19

LOB, OR SCREEN AND ROLL

The offside forward, (4), keys this play when he notices (1) cannot get the ball inside. He does so by stepping up and screening for the offside guard, (2), who cuts to the basket for a possible lob pass from (1). See Diagram 8-20.

If (2) is not open, (3) clears across the high-post area to screen for (4) who comes to the ballside. At the same time, (1) and (5) work a screen-and-roll play on the clear side. See Diagram 8-21.

If neither (1) nor (5) are open, (4) might lose his man on

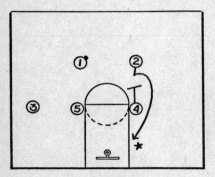

Diagram 8-20

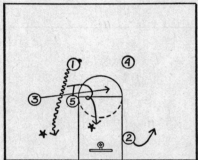

Diagram 8-21

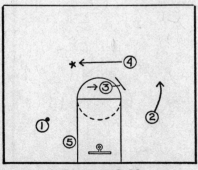

Diagram 8-22

(3)'s screen for a jump shot at the free throw line. See Diagram 8-22.

(2) maintains defensive balance by swinging out front.

GUARDS CROSS, FORWARDS CROSS

When guard, (1), cannot get the ball inside, he dribbles toward (2), passes the ball to him, and they cross. This tells the forwards to cross and usually one of them is open. See Diagrams 8-23 and 8-24.

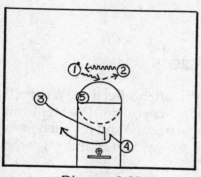

Diagram 8-23

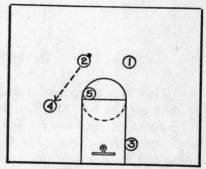

Diagram 8-24

DRIBBLE ENTRY

This simple play is executed by the guard with the ball, (1), dribbling at his overplayed forward, (3), and clearing him. At times, (3) may be open on a backdoor-type move for a bounce pass and lay-up shot. See Diagram 8-25.

If (3) is not open, he clears across the lane and (1) is now in the forward position with the ball. The offside guard, (2), swings to the ballside and a play may be run. See Diagram 8-26.

(3) maintains defensive balance by moving out to the offside guard position.

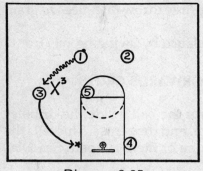
Diagram 8-25

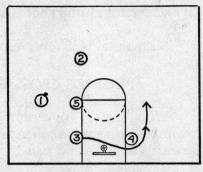
Diagram 8-26

INVERT CROSS

This is a simple play that is often effective. When (1) cannot get the ball to (3), the high-post man, (5), steps out high and receives from (1). Both guards, (1) and (2), then go in and screen for their respective forwards, (3) and (4), who come out front. See Diagram 8-27.

(5) then passes to one of the forwards and returns to his high-post area. The guards cross inside, and the forward with the ball makes the penetration pass to start a play. The guards and forward have changed positions. See Diagrams 8-28 and 8-29 for illustrations of these plays.

This pressure reliever works very well because the defensive guards and forwards have also changed positions and may be unfamiliar with their assignments.

These ideas are not necessarily scoring plays. They are designed to get the ball inside versus pressure. For a given team, only one or two of them would be needed. They are answers for those times when you play against an overplaying, pressuring, man-to-man defense.

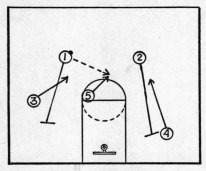

Diagram 8-27

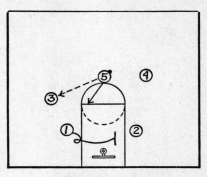

Diagram 8-28

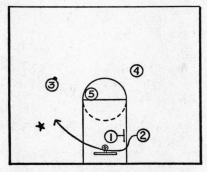

Diagram 8-29

9

VERSUS ZONE DEFENSES

Many of the plays mentioned in previous chapters can, with some slight adjustments, be used against zone defenses. Some of them are described in this chapter.

THE BASIC DOUBLE-CUT PLAY

(1) passes to (3), cuts off the post man and down and around the offside forward, (4). The offside guard, (2), then cuts off the post and to the ballside low-post area. See Diagram 9-1.

Play continues as (3) passes to (5), stepping to the head of the key. At this point several zone possibilities have occurred. The front of the zone offense has changed from even to odd and will now split an even-front zone. A couple of cutters, (1) and (2), have gone through the zone, and it is now possible to reverse the ball to (1) behind (4)'s zone screening move. After (3) passes to (5), he can pinch down to trap the zone inside and provide a jump shot for (2), popping out to the side. See Diagram 9-2.

As soon as a pass is made from (5) to either wing, the offside inside man cuts to the free throw line area. If he

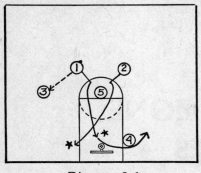

Diagram 9-1

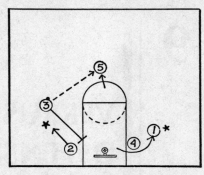

Diagram 9-2

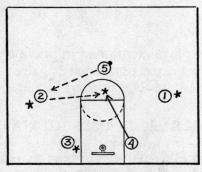

Diagram 9-3

receives a pass, he can shoot or look inside for the man in the low-post area. See Diagram 9-3.

In Diagram 9-3, the ball can also be passed from (4) to (1) in the offside wing area.

POST EXCHANGE PLAY

When running the post exchange play versus zone defenses, guard (1), as before, passes to his forward, (3), and cuts through, but this time he goes only halfway to the corner. Post man, (5), instead of making a diagonal cut to screen for

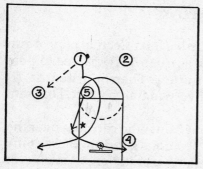

Diagram 9-4

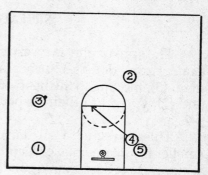

Diagram 9-5

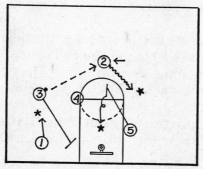

Diagram 9-6

(4), drops down to the ballside low-post area and then crosses the lane. See Diagram 9-4.

Continuing the pattern, offside forward, (4), cuts to the ballside of the free throw line. If (3) passes to (4), he may shoot or look for (5) inside the zone. See Diagram 9-5.

If (3) cannot pass to (5), sliding down, or (4), cutting to the ball, (2) moves toward him and receives a pass. After the pass, (3) tries to trap the zone inside by screening down for (1). (2) may pass to (1), or use the screen set by (5) to dribble away for a jump shot. (5) rolls for rebounding position in Diagram 9-6.

SPREAD PLAY

The spread play is a very simple but effective play to run against zone defenses. It begins as guard, (1), passes to post man, (5), moving to the head of the key. Then both guards, (1) and (2), spread to their respective wing areas. See Diagram 9-7.

This move puts a tall man out front who can pass over the smaller front zone players, and positions good shooters at the wing areas where many good shots usually are available. If this maneuver spreads the defense, (5) whips a two-hand overhead pass to either (3) or (4) inside, or passes to the open wing and makes an exchange with the offside forward. See Diagram 9-8.

When (5) passes to (1), it changes the defensive angle on (3) and often allows (1) to get the ball inside.

If (4) is open at the free throw line, (1) passes to him and (4) can shoot or look for (3) and (5) inside the zone. See Diagram 9-9.

If not open, (4) continues out front, (1) passes to him and the original play potential exists again. See Diagram 9-10.

GUARD LOOP PLAY

Guard, (1), passes to forward, (3), and makes a looping cut around high-post man, (5). The offside guard, (2), follows (1) over (5) and continues down, across the lane, and around the offside forward, (4). (3) may now:

a. Pass to (5) as he slides down the lane to the ballside low-post area as shown in Diagram 9-11.

b. Reverse the ball to (2) by way of (1). When this option is used, (4) attempts to pin the zone inside by screening the zone player nearest to him as in Diagram 9-12.

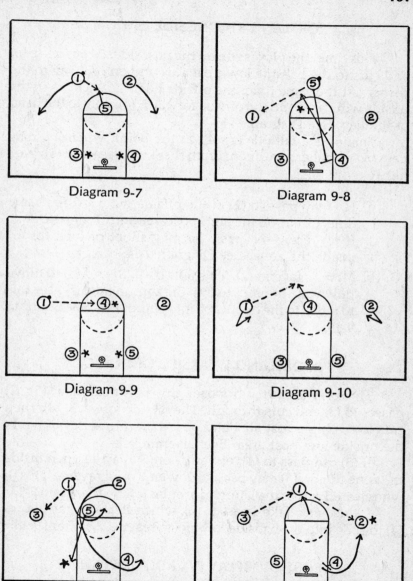

Diagram 9-7

Diagram 9-8

Diagram 9-9

Diagram 9-10

Diagram 9-11

Diagram 9-12

PORTLAND STRONGSIDE OPTION

This time, the play is run on the post side. (1) passes to (3) and cuts to the ballside low-post area and on halfway to the corner. At the same time, the offside guard, (2), clears to the offside wing area and the offside forward, (4), cuts to the head of the key. See Diagram 9-13.

This puts a tall player, (4), at the point, where he may pass over smaller zone men. From there, (3) passes to (4), who has two options:

a.   He may pass to (2) at the offside wing. At the same time, (3) cuts to the high-post area and (5) slides down. If (3) receives a pass, he may shoot or look for (5) inside the zone. See Diagram 9-14.

b.   (4) may fake to (2). This tells both (3) and (5) to move down and attempt to trap the zone inside. (1) uses this to move to the open area for a jump shot. See Diagram 9-15.

PORTLAND WEAKSIDE OPTION

This play is started opposite the high-post man, (5). (1) passes to (3) and cuts through. The offside forward, (4), then cuts to the high-post area and post man, (5), slides down to the offside low-post area. See Diagram 9-16.

If (3) can pass to (4), either (1) or (5) may be open inside the zone. If not, (3) may pass to (2) who would reverse it to (1), who cleared across the lane and around (5). See Diagram 9-17.

(3) also may fake a pass to (2), which clears (1) and allows (4) to slide into the ballside low-post area. See Diagram 9-18.

POST OVERPLAY BACKDOOR PLAY

There is not much chance that a backdoor play will work well against zones. However, the movement involved in this play is functional versus zone defenses.

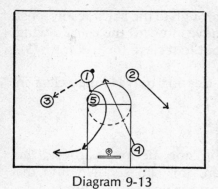

Diagram 9-13

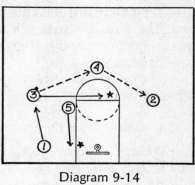

Diagram 9-14

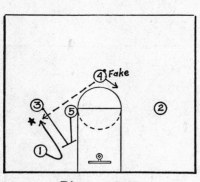

Diagram 9-15

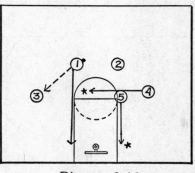

Diagram 9-16

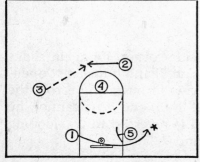

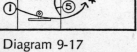

Diagram 9-17

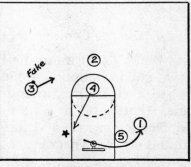

Diagram 9-18

(1) passes to (3) and cuts through to the ballside low-post area. The offside guard, (2), moves toward the offside wing area and post man, (5), steps out to receive the ball from (3). See Diagram 9-19.

(1) then keys the play by clearing out. He may clear in either of two ways:

A. Clear Across the Lane

When (1) clears across the lane, he loops around the offside forward, (4). Post man, (5), slides down into the ballside low-post area and is a possible option. (2) moves to the point, receives the ball from (3), and passes to (1) coming around (4). See Diagram 9-20.

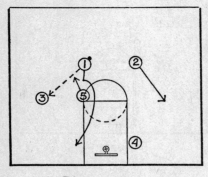 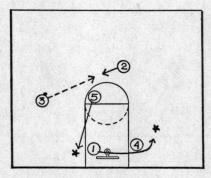

Diagram 9-19   Diagram 9-20

B. Clear to Corner

When (1) clears to the ballside corner, (5) again slides down and is an option. (3) looks at (5) and if he is not open, passes to (1) in the corner and cuts through and across the lane. (1) attempts to get the ball to (5) and if he cannot, he dribbles toward (2) and the ball is reversed to (3), looping around (4). See Diagrams 9-21 and 9-22.

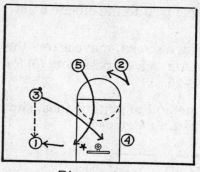

Diagram 9-21

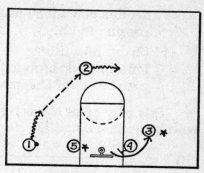

Diagram 9-22

HIGH CLEAR SLASH PLAY

This is a play designed to get the last-second shot for (2), the best shooter on the team. (1) dribbles at (3) and clears him around (5) and to the point. At the same time, (2) cuts to the ballside low-post area. See Diagram 9-23.

(1) then passes to (3) and one of two things may happen:

a. (1) screens down for (2) and traps the zone inside to give (2) a jump shot as shown in Diagram 9-24. (3) can

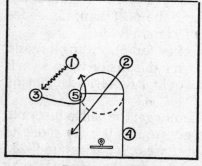

Diagram 9-23

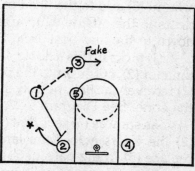

Diagram 9-24

set this play up by faking a pass to the offside before passing to (2).

  b. (2) can fake using (1)'s down screen, move across the lane and loop around (4) to receive a pass from (3) for the shot as in Diagram 9-25.

This play gives a coach a method of getting a last shot with his best shooter, (2), versus zone defenses.

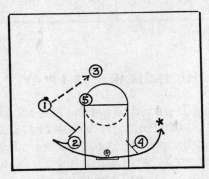

Diagram 9-25

HIGH CLEAR POST DOWN PLAY

This play begins when (1) dribbles at (3) and clears him around (5) and to the head of the key. The offside guard, (2), clears to the offside wing area, and the post man, (5), slides down to the low-post area. See Diagram 9-26.

(1) picks up his dribble, looks first for (5), cutting low and then for (2), cutting into the post from the offside wing area. If (2) receives the ball, he may shoot or look for (4) and (5) inside the zone. See Diagram 9-27.

As soon as (5) sees that (1) cannot get the ball to him or to (2), he clears across the lane and around (4). (2) slides to replace (5) in the ballside low-post area. See Diagram 9-28.

(1) may pass to (2) sliding down, or reverse it to (5) by way of (3). See Diagram 9-29.

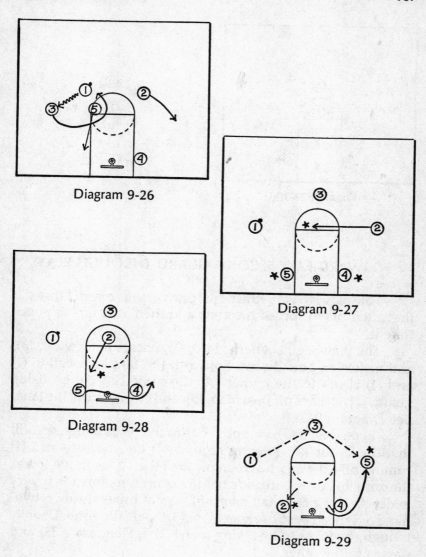

Diagram 9-26

Diagram 9-27

Diagram 9-28

Diagram 9-29

If (5) receives the ball and cannot shoot, (1) cuts to the high-post area and the same options are available. See Diagrams 9-30 and 9-31.

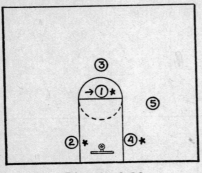

Diagram 9-30

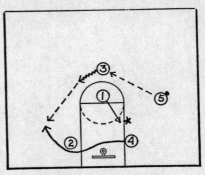

Diagram 9-31

FORWARD FAKE SECOND GUARD THROUGH PLAY

This play is a very functional one versus zone defenses. It first attempts to spread the zone and then attempts to penetrate it.

The play begins when guard, (1), passes to forward, (3), and makes an outside cut. Forward, (3), fakes the ball to (1) and (1) clears to the corner. At the same time, the offside guard, (2), slashes off post man, (5), and clears across the lane. See Diagram 9-32.

(3) passes to (5), stepping out to the head of the key. (5) then looks for (2), looping around (4) on one side and (1) coming off (3)'s down screen on the other. This move forces the zone to cover both sides of the court and spreads it very wide. At this point, tall man, (5), can at times throw a two-hand overhead pass to either (4) or (3) inside the zone. Usually though, he fakes to one wing man [(2) in Diagram 9-33] and passes to the other.

When this happens, (2) now cuts quickly to the center high-post area. (1) may shoot or pass to (2) in the middle. (2) could then shoot or look inside for (3) or (4). See Diagram 9-34.

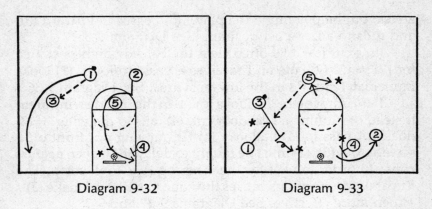

Diagram 9-32   Diagram 9-33

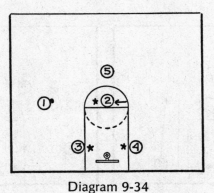

Diagram 9-34

THE DOUBLE DOWN BACKDOOR PLAY

This play works well against zones because it offers an opportunity to get the ball to the high-post area and then quickly to the low-post area. This action is very difficult for zones to defend.

As in previous plays, (1) passes to (5) in the high-post area. Guards (1) and (2) exchange with their respective forwards. (This exchange does not accomplish much against zones, but helps to time the play.) (5) passes to forward (3), and rolls to a low-post position. See Diagram 9-35.

(5)'s cut low will often clear the ballside high-post area for (2)'s cut. (2) cuts and receives a pass from (3). (2) looks immediately for (5) in the low-post area. See Diagram 9-36.

If (5) is not open, (2) looks for (4) in the offside wing area. Instead of running a backdoor cut, (4) fans to the wing. If (2) does not pass to (4) he looks for (1), moving out front off a screen from (3). (3) must be taught to delay the screen against zones in order to wait for the other options to develop. The threat of these options causes the zone to shift and make (3)'s screen more effective. See Diagrams 9-37 and 9-38.

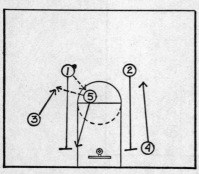

Diagram 9-35

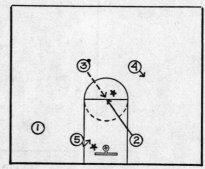

Diagram 9-36

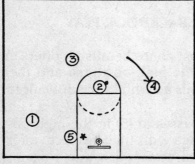

Diagram 9-37

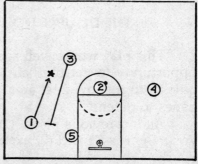

Diagram 9-38

10

EVALUATING THE PRO-SET OFFENSE

When evaluating any offense, the first thing you must do is take a long look at the personnel available to you. One way to do this is to rate them in terms of: (a) speed and quickness, (b) size, and (c) shooting ability. This rating, of course, should be done in comparison to the opposition they must face. Most strong players have at least two of these traits. Then, within the framework of this evaluation and within the confines of your basketball coaching philosophy, you must seek techniques that best utilize the talents of your players and hide their apparent weaknesses.

The pro-set offense, as it is presented here, contains a very wide variety of offensive maneuvers. This abundance of alternatives should allow you to find plays that relate well to your situation.

These plays are also designed with consideration to the fundamentals of man-to-man offense. They are as follows:

I. GETTING A PERCENTAGE SHOT

Moving the post man to the high-post area above the free throw line opens up the ballside lay-up slot areas and results in more easy shots close to the basket. See Diagram 10-1. The post man is also in excellent position to "feed" the low-post area. This allows the forwards to move in tight and "post up" their opponents. See Diagram 10-2.

Utilizing the high forward area (free throw line extended) as a primary passing area puts much pressure on the defense. They must cover the low post, high post, and the head of the key. See Diagram 10-3.

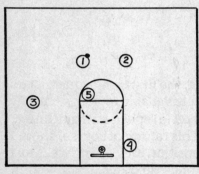

Diagram 10-1

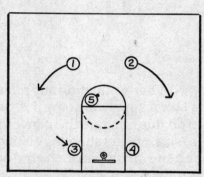

Diagram 10-2

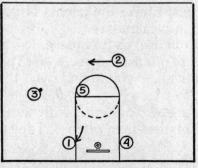

Diagram 10-3

Another factor that comes into play is that the big defensive post man must play high, and this takes away much of the defense's shot-blocking potential. Eliminating these blocked shots and the fear of having a shot blocked raises the shooting percentage.

II. GETTING THE SECOND SHOT

When using the pro-set offense, a high percentage of the shots are taken within twelve feet of the basket. This cuts down the rebound advantage of the defense. Also, the defensive post man is forced to cover a high-post player. As a result, he must move to attain good rebound position. When using the pro-set offense, the inside offensive men must charge the boards on every shot. They must learn to anticipate the offensive shot options, and be aware that the guards have the primary responsibility for defensive balance.

III. MAINTAINING DEFENSIVE BALANCE

There are a great many plays in this book, but in general, when one guard goes inside, the other is responsible for defensive balance. An example is shown in Diagram 10-4.

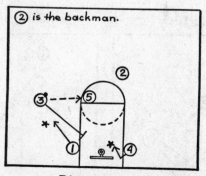

Diagram 10-4

When they both go through, as in the double-cut plays, the guard away from the play and/or high is the player with the primary responsibility for defensive balance. See Diagram 10-5. These responsibilities must be worked on in practice to clear up all doubts.

IV. MEETING DEFENSIVE PRESSURE

Chapter 8 deals with this subject by providing pressure-relieving maneuvers. Some of the necessary offensive counters to defensive pressure are backdoor plays, dribble entry plays, guard-to-guard plays, and lob plays. All are provided in this book.

It is also very helpful if the offense has a functional shape from which to meet pressure. This offense has a 2-1-2 shape and the position of the high-post man allows for an easy pass any time. The guards are double-teamed. See Diagram 10-6.

It is very wise for a team's zone pressure offense to have the same alignment as their basic man-to-man and zone offenses. This permits the team to move quickly into its pressure offense to meet surprise pressure. If their offensive alignment must be changed to meet pressure, the team is placed at a

Diagram 10-5

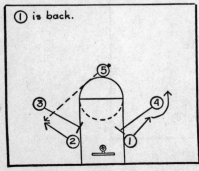

Diagram 10-6

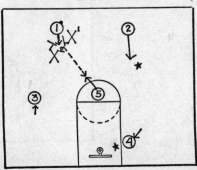

disadvantage until it can attain the proper formation. The 2-1-2 alignment is an ideal shape from which double-teaming pressure can be countered.

V. HAVING THE PROPER AMOUNT OF MOVEMENT

This, of course, will depend on the personnel. In general, it is wise for a team that is not as strong in rebounding as the opposition is to move on offense. Conversely, a superior rebounding team may find offensive movement a negative factor.

Movement also takes time. A team that runs a patient continuity-type offense may have trouble catching up when time is running out. Ideally, every team should have some quick-hitter plays in short-time situations and a continuity to run when they want to be patient and use the clock.

Movement can also be used as a maneuvering device. A coach may want to run a play that maneuvers a big defensive center out of the rebounding area and then provides for a quick shot.

The wide assortment of plays in this book allows you to choose those that provide functional movement for your particular coaching situation.

VI. UTILIZING BASIC PLAYS

A successful offense should contain a variety of play situations. Some of the basic plays used in this book are the: screen-and-roll, pass and screen-away, post-splitting, give-and-go, backdoor, down screen and stack, clearouts, natural screens, wall plays, isolation, reversals, and wheel plays. You should look at all of them and—after relating them to your team's size, talents, fundamental background, patience, discipline, intelligence, stamina, attention span, time to develop, and even weaknesses—choose those which best fit your situation.

This X and O search should always be tempered by the stark realization that games are won by players and not plays. Your final choice should be the minimum of plays that will permit your players to execute them comfortably and still present the opposition with a challenging variety of play situations.

VII. DISCIPLINED FLEXIBILITY

Discipline is necessary in an offense to assure that good percentage shots are taken from the right areas at the most opportune time by the proper individuals. Flexibility must be allowed in order for the players to spontaneously respond to defensive counters in a manner that utilizes their talents to the utmost. There are plays in this book that permit a team the options of being guard-oriented, forward-oriented, and post-oriented, or that provide an equal shot distribution among the various positions.

VIII. BEING ABLE TO ADAPT TO ZONE DEFENSES

Just having a man-to-man offense and a zone offense is not enough. All or some of your man-to-man offense must also work against zone defenses. Following are some of the situations in which this attribute will be of help:

a. When the opposition is changing defenses. Many teams play man-to-man after they have not scored on offense and zone after they have scored.

b. When the opposition is playing a combination defense, such as a box and one or diamond and one.

c. When the opposition plays a man-to-man defense that has zone principles.

    d. When the opposition plays a zone that has man-to-man principles.

    e. When your zone offense is ineffective and you need some alternative.

Chapter 9 gives examples of man-to-man plays adapted to work against zone defenses.

IX. UTILIZING PLAY KEYS

In basketball, offensive plays may be called by hand signals, oral signals, formations, or by a pass and cut key. The latter is probably the most often used, and most mechanically functional. Each of the first seven chapters consists of plays called by a particular pass and cut, or dribble key. The three basic keys for this offense are the inside cut, the outside cut, and the pass-to-the-post play. The other four may be added when needed. The dribble entry play and the guard-to-guard play are helpful versus strong defensive pressure. The diagonal cut facilitates using a strong post man and the double-cut play should be considered by a guard-oriented team.

X. TAKING ADVANTAGE OF PERSONNEL MATCH-UPS

After you have designed your offense to best fit your personnel, there is still the problem of game-to-game personnel match-ups. One answer to this is to make a decision as to what will work best in a given week and then tell your quarterbacking guard the plays that should be featured and those that should be played down. On top of this, it might be wise to design a specific play or plays that best takes advantage of the personnel match-ups. One of the great basketball coaches, Ramon Mears, used to do this when he coached at Wittenberg

College and Tennessee University. He would name the week's special play after the opposing school's team name. The Kentucky University play should be "The Wildcat," the Ohio State University play "The Buckeye," and so on. These special plays also gave his teams a psychological edge because they knew they were designed to put the percentages in their favor. In the event these plays were very successful, Coach Mears would come back to them later in the season in fairly similar circumstances.

In closing, I would like to repeat that games are not won by plays but by players. The coach's choice of offensive team techniques, however, must be such that they allow each player to do what he does best in the context of a team game.

Index